Contents

01 | Understanding what history means

History = the past, the study of the past.

The story of your life until now is your history. The word 'history' comes from a Greek word meaning 'knowledge got by inquiry'.

The Father of History is Herodotus. He lived in Ancient Greece and died about 425 BCE (Before the Common Era or Before Christ). He wanted to find out what caused a war between Greeks and Persians. Persia is the old name for the country of Iran. Herodotus travelled all around the area and asked questions. Then he wrote down the events that had happened and tried to explain why they happened. That is the first history the world knows about.

Sometimes students groan when they hear the word history. They think history is a collection of dates they have to learn off by heart. Dates can be important. For example, you will use the date of the year you were born many times throughout your life. But history is all about finding things out and thinking about what has happened to create the world in which you now live.

1 State four differences between you and Herodotus.

a _____

b _____

c _____

d _____

2 Relate the image to what history means and what you do as a history student.

_____

_____

_____

_____

 ISBN: 9780170389334

Understanding what historical information is

> Historical information = knowledge got through research and inquiry.

THE LANDING of the CONVICTS at BOTANY BAY

Example

One of Kip's ancestors was 13 years old when the English transported her to a convict settlement in Australia for trying to steal bread to feed her starving family. Kip knows this because the event was recorded in official records, in the front page of the family Bible which has been handed down the generations, and on a family tree made by a professional.

Historical information is also about historical ideas – things you realise or understand after you have checked out all the facts.

Example

Sean has Irish ancestors. He has heard them talk of the dark days when England ruled Ireland and tried to get rid of everything Irish such as language and hairstyles, and how the Irish fought back. A family story says the English had pitch-capped one member of Sean's family by pouring pitch (tar) on his head, putting gunpowder on the pitch and setting the head on fire. Sean imagines what it would be like to have his head on fire and now he has an understanding of a historical idea – that the historical relationship between Ireland and England had not always been friendly.

CAP.ⁿ SWAYNE
Pitch Capping the People of Prosperous

1 State two things that historical information is about.

a _____

b _____

2 Finish the following to give two pieces of historical information about yourself.

a When I was young, I watched _____

b Earlier this year, I went to _____

3 Give four historical facts you have learned in this unit.

_____

_____

_____

_____

03 | Understanding where history happens

All around the world, right now, history is being made. History happens everywhere. That is why you need to know roughly where places and countries are.

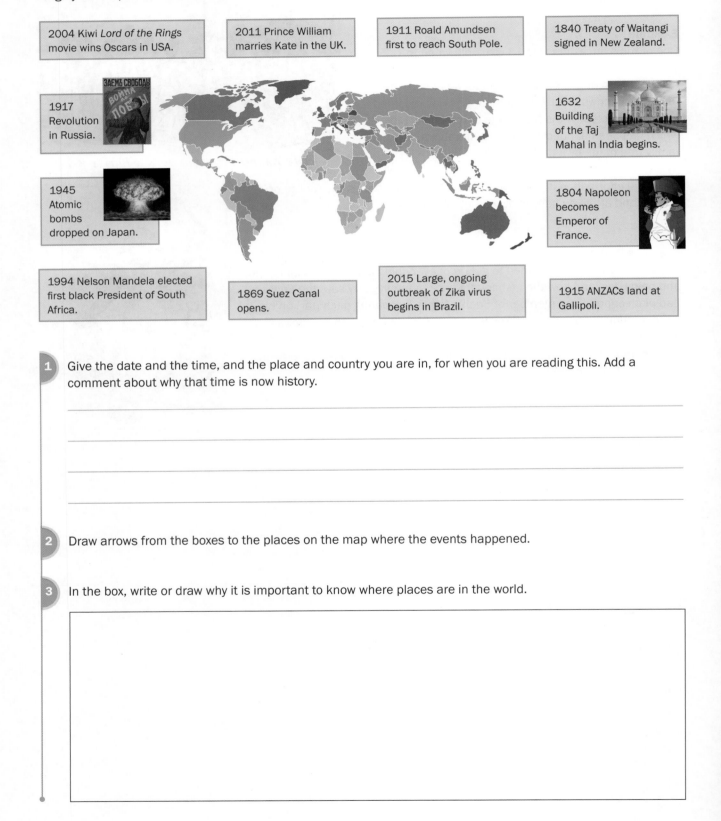

2004 Kiwi *Lord of the Rings* movie wins Oscars in USA.

2011 Prince William marries Kate in the UK.

1911 Roald Amundsen first to reach South Pole.

1840 Treaty of Waitangi signed in New Zealand.

1917 Revolution in Russia.

1632 Building of the Taj Mahal in India begins.

1945 Atomic bombs dropped on Japan.

1804 Napoleon becomes Emperor of France.

1994 Nelson Mandela elected first black President of South Africa.

1869 Suez Canal opens.

2015 Large, ongoing outbreak of Zika virus begins in Brazil.

1915 ANZACs land at Gallipoli.

1 Give the date and the time, and the place and country you are in, for when you are reading this. Add a comment about why that time is now history.

2 Draw arrows from the boxes to the places on the map where the events happened.

3 In the box, write or draw why it is important to know where places are in the world.

 ISBN: 9780170389334

Social history = people being part of society, such as doing jobs to make a living.

Social historians look at all the different types of people doing this, such as:

astronauts	beauty therapists	c
d	e	firefighters
games developers	h	i
job analysts	kiwifruit pickers	lifeguards
midwives	n	o
pastry chefs	quality technicians	r
s	tattooists	ushers
v	w	X-ray technicians
youth workers	zoologists	

Occupations

Social history looks at every feature of society such as:

architecture	bungy-jumping	computers	data gathering	e
families	games	holidays	inventions	jazz
k	laws	medicines	names	online time
p	queens	r	s	technology
universities	vehicles	welfare	xenophobia	yetis
zoos				

Features of society

1 Name five people alive today, famous or ordinary, whom you think would make good subjects for a history project.

2 Finish the charts of examples of occupations and features of society.

3 List 10 topics that you might be interested in researching for a social history project.

Knowing the 5 Ws and H of history

History answers, or tries to answer, questions about:

WHO   Who won the rugby World Cup in 2015?
(New Zealand)

WHAT   What animals helped Hannibal get his army over the Alps in 218 BCE to attack the Roman Empire?
(elephants)

WHERE   Where did building of a Great Wall begin as early as the 7th century BCE?
(China)

WHEN   When did Turners and Growers change the name of Chinese gooseberries to kiwifruit?
(1959)

WHY   Why do people in the USA still talk of 9/11?
(Four terrorist attacks by Islamic group on USA 11 September 2001.)

HOW   Adds extra information such as:

- In what manner? How did President Lincoln die?
  (assassination)
- In what condition? How was Elizabeth I after she had Mary Queen of Scots executed?
  (Indignant; she had given vague orders so she could not be said to be fully responsible)
- To what extent? How many wives did Henry VIII have?
  (six)
- At what price? How many people died in the Second World War?
  (over 60 million)
- For what reason? How is it that your family lives in this country and not some other country?

    ISBN: 9780170389334

One of the first places the Boxing Day tsunami hit was an island near Sumatra. It swept away thousands of people including 13-year-old Meghna. She survived in the ocean for two days by clinging to a drifting door. Because she knew in which direction the land lay, she floated towards the shore. Helicopters failed to spot her. Finally, waves washed her ashore. She was badly bruised and dazed. Locals found her and got her airlifted to hospital where she recovered.

1 Fill in the missing answer to the 'How' question about how your family came to be living here.

2 Draw arrows from the six boxes above the tsunami story to show to which parts of the story they refer.

3 The rhyming verse below is from Rudyard Kipling (1865-1936) who wrote famous jungle stories featuring a Royal Bengal Tiger and a boy raised by wolves. Work out what the three missing words are likely to be and write them in.

> I keep six honest serving men
>
> They taught me all I knew
>
> Their names are What and Why and _____
>
> And How and _____ and _____

4 Use the 5 Ws and H to write six short questions about the 2016 Olympic Games.

a _____

b _____

c _____

d _____

e _____

f _____

06 | Understanding oral history

Example

Early in 2016 the first group of 82 Syrians arrived at the Mangere refugee centre in Auckland. The New Zealand government had decided to take 600 extra Syrians on top of its annual quota of 750 refugees. Syrian refugees had oral histories to tell – of the war in their country, which forced them to flee their homes and find another country in which to live.

oral = spoken, the opposite of written

oral history = a person talking about an event or time he or she lived through and which is recorded, usually electronically.

Syrian refugees in a refugee camp in Jordan.

Oral histories are

- about events that happened in real life rather than in imaginations
- people talking about their life experiences
- another way to learn about the past
- voices from oral cultures, such as pre-European Maori
- personal recollections
- sources of information for radio and television programmes, in museums and on the net
- presented as evidence in courts such as in land claims
- a way for cultures to pass on knowledge
- from the point of view of the people relating them
- historical evidence about the past.

1 Give an event from your life, past or present or future, that might make an interesting oral history.

_____

2 Say why oral history can do the following.

a Give people a sense of worth. _____

_____

b Make a historical event more exciting. _____

_____

c Make people ask for proof that the event happened. ____

_____

3 Name people who might be able to talk to you about the following.

a The day you were born. _____

b The day in 2011 when an earthquake hit Christchurch. ____

_____

 ISBN: 9780170389334

Understanding local community

Local is
- from a Latin word meaning place
- to do with a small area rather than the whole country.

Community is
- from Latin words meaning common
- a group of people living in a place.

Local community is
- an area such as a small town or suburb
- a group of interacting people sharing an environment.

Every natural and man-made feature such as hill, waterway, road, farm, private house and public building has an individual history, while the local community as a whole has a shared history.

You may be asked to do a special study of an important historic building or construction in your local community. You could choose something like an old house, or a wall of plaques that commemorates local soldiers who fought in wars overseas.

Examples of questions to answer to show why your building or construction is important:

- When was it built?
- Who uses it?
- Why was it built?
- What is its function?
- Where is it located?
- How does it look today?

1 Say how this local community is like or different to your local community.

_____

_____

_____

_____

_____

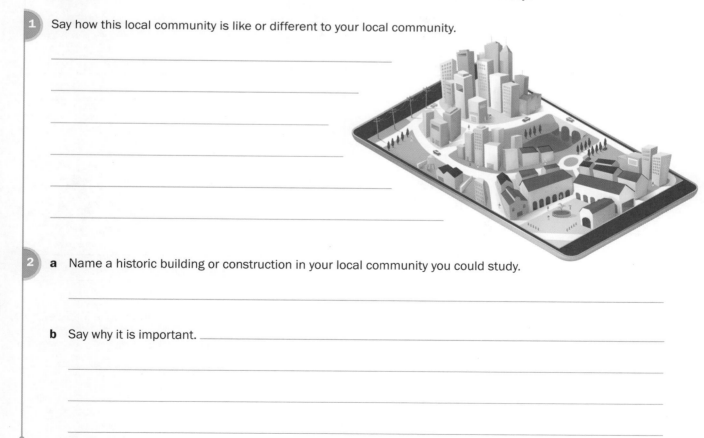

2 **a** Name a historic building or construction in your local community you could study.

_____

b Say why it is important. _____

_____

_____

_____

How to create oral history

Decide on the issue you want to research, e.g. *What was it like in the time before mobile phones?*
Think of what people might remember such as how they communicated with friends.
Create 10 questions that could get information on the issue, e.g. *What other technology did you not have that is available today?*
Use questions that need more than a Yes/No answer, e.g. Instead of '*Do you think mobiles have improved society?*' ask '*In what ways did the lack of mobiles make life different?*'
Find someone to interview. The first mobiles arrived in New Zealand in 1985 with analogue technology.
Phone, write or visit to introduce yourself. Give your name, age, class and school. Describe the issue you are researching. Ask if you can record the conversation. Ask if you can share the information you gather, such as writing it up for a class report or a project for your teacher to assess.

Rules for good interview manners
1 Be on time.
2 Be ready – questions organised, recording equipment working.
3 Be polite. Say 'please' and 'thank you'.
4 Be respectful. Call the person by title such as Mrs or Grandfather.
5 Be patient.
6 Listen without arguing or correcting the speaker.
7 Listen carefully and show interest in what the person is saying.
8 Write down any follow-up questions that might arise from what the person is saying and ask them later.
9 Thank the person.
10 You might like to send a thank you note or email later, or a copy of your written-up material for the person to keep.

1 Under each image, put one or more numbers to show which rules for good interview manners the interviewer is breaking.

2 In the box, write or draw how oral history is made.

 ISBN: 9780170389334

Knowing about artefacts

Artefacts (also 'artifacts')

- are objects such as tools or works of art made by humans
- usually come from the past so are called old-fashioned, retro, vintage, antique
- have a history such as where and when they were made
- can tell you about how people lived at that particular time.

1 In the boxes below the images, put what you think these artefacts are.

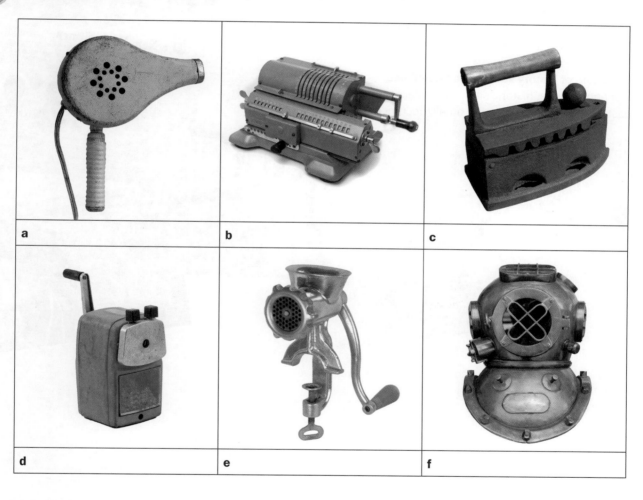

a

b

c

d

e

f

2 Name five objects from your home that a historian in 50 years' time might call artefacts and be excited to see.

_____

_____

_____

_____

_____

10 | Understanding what sources are

Sources	= sometimes called resources
	= places or things from which something comes
	= something that is available for help when needed.

Examples

- The source of the story about the politician's past affair was a diary.
- The Ancients did not know the source of the River Nile.
- He used sources such as old newspapers to learn about the First World War.
- Sources she included in her PowerPoint on Gallipoli included maps, letters and cartoons.

Examples of history sources you could use

Museum, marae, historic site, library, field trip, internet, cemetery, chart, poster, photograph, postcard, email, document, text message, report.

1. Name the sources in each of the seven pictures above.

_____

_____

_____

_____

2. Name four traces of your activities this week, such as some dated schoolwork or net history, that you may leave behind to become a historical source.

_____

_____

_____

_____

  ISBN: 9780170389334

Knowing the difference between primary and secondary sources

A primary source

* comes first and is original
* is first-hand evidence or a contemporary account of an event, person or object created by someone who was alive at the time
* is something like an eyewitness report, a speech, a document, an artefact, a photograph, a newspaper story, an interview, a diary, a letter.

A secondary source

* comes after a primary source, maybe hundreds of years later
* is a second-hand view of an event, person or object
* interprets and comments about primary sources
* is something like a textbook, a journal, an essay, an editorial, a website.

1 In the blank boxes put either P (for primary) or S (for secondary) to show what type of source each is.

a Over 150 years ago, in April 1865, US President Abraham Lincoln was assassinated at a theatre while he was watching a play. The assassin jumped out of the President's box on to the stage. He fled into the night but was killed several days later by soldiers.

b

Assassination of Lincoln published in April 1865.

c

Bicycle messengers in 1900.

d In 1900 early couriers, known as bicycle messengers, rode penny-farthing bikes, which had large front wheels and small back wheels. Such messengers would be amazed at today's high-tech delivery systems.

2 The following are sources to do with the storming of Bastille prison in Paris on 14 July 1789 and its destruction. Put P (for primary) or S (for secondary) beside each one.

a ☐ Sketch from 14 July 1789 of the prison moat and eight towers.

b ☐ A history, written in 2016, of the prison from the time of its creation in the 1300s.

c ☐ A photograph of people celebrating Bastille Day in 2015.

d ☐ A priest's eye-witness account of the mob attacking the prison.

e ☐ An entry in an 1899 encyclopaedia about the event.

f ☐ A diary entry from that day of the mob parading victims' heads on poles.

Understanding what statistics are

> Statistics = collecting and analysing data.
> Data = facts such as numbers, measurements, observations.
> Statistics New Zealand (Tatauranga Aotearoa) = department that collects and produces statistics.

Example 1

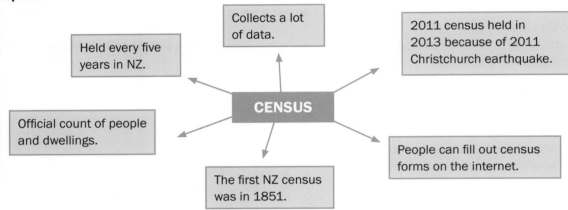

Held every five years in NZ.

Collects a lot of data.

2011 census held in 2013 because of 2011 Christchurch earthquake.

CENSUS

Official count of people and dwellings.

People can fill out census forms on the internet.

The first NZ census was in 1851.

Example 2

Statisticians used data from the 2013 census to work out what New Zealand would be like as a village of 100 people.

- 4,242,048 was the resident population so each person represented 42,420 people.
- 49 people were male and 51 were female.
- The village's population had tripled in the last 87 years.
- 70 people were European, 14 were Maori, 11 were Asian.
- 70 people were born in New Zealand.
- 7 were born in Asia, and 6 were born in the United Kingdom and Ireland.
- 4 were born in the Pacific Islands and 2 were born in the Middle East and Africa.
- 2 were born in Europe (excluding the UK and Ireland) and 1 was born in Australia.
- 1 was born in North America and 6 had unknown birthplaces.
- 80 people were aged 15 and over.
- 4 in 5 people aged 15 and over had a formal qualification.
- 10 were professionals, 8 were managers, 5 were clerical and admin workers, 5 were technicians and trades workers, 5 were labourers, 4 were community and personal service workers, 4 were sales workers and 2 were machinery operators and drivers.
- 4 earned $100,001 or more, and 38 earned $30,000 and less.

Example 3

From the 2014 Ministry of Health statistics for children and young people:

- Nearly half of children aged 5–14 years (45%) usually used active transport (eg. walking, cycling) to get to and from school.
- Nearly half of children aged 5–14 years (50%) usually watched 2 or more hours of television a day, down from 57% in 2006/07.
- 28% of secondary school students watched television for 3 or more hours each day.
- 35% of secondary school students went on the internet for 3 or more hours each day.
- 32% of male secondary school students played games for 3 or more hours each day.
- 9% of female secondary school students played games for 3 or more hours each day.
- The proportion of students watching more than 1 hour of TV each day dropped from 73% in 2007 to 65% in 2012.
- 10% of students met the current recommendations of 60 minutes of physical activity daily.

ISBN: 9780170389334

Example 4

Using data from summer Olympic gold medals up to and including 2012, in terms of medal numbers per one million, population rankings for the top 10 countries in order were Finland, Hungary, Sweden, Bahamas, Norway, Grenada, East Germany, New Zealand, Denmark, Estonia. This put New Zealand ahead of countries like Australia, the USA, Canada and the UK.

1

Loading punch cards into tabulating machine used in the 1920 US census. It mechanically read punch cards with coded information. New Zealand imported some tabulating machines from the US in the 1920s for its census statistical work and in time these were replaced with mainframe computers, microcomputers and the internet.

Comment on how technology has made working with statistics more user-friendly.

_____

_____

_____

_____

_____

_____

_____

2 Supply short answers to the following.

a Maori name for Statistics New Zealand _____

b How often New Zealand holds a census _____

c When New Zealand first held a census _____

d What processed and stored information for a tabulating machine _____

e New Zealand's resident population in 2013 _____

3 Supply longer answers to the following.

a How New Zealand made it into the Top Ten for the number of Olympic gold medals.

_____

b A 2014 statistic that shows a difference in digital use between genders.

_____

c A 2014 statistic that shows a low percentage meeting a recommendation.

_____

d A 2013 statistic that shows a difference in earnings.

_____

e A 2013 statistic that shows a gender imbalance in population.

_____

13 | Using diagrams

Diagrams displaying historical data give instant overviews and summaries of a topic.
Diagramming software can generate many of the different types of diagrams, or you can create your own.

Example 1 Pyramid

- The most important goes at the top of the pyramid.
- The shape of the pyramid shows how there are fewer of the top class than there are of the bottom class.

Social classes of Victorian England

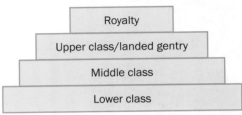

Example 2 Star diagram

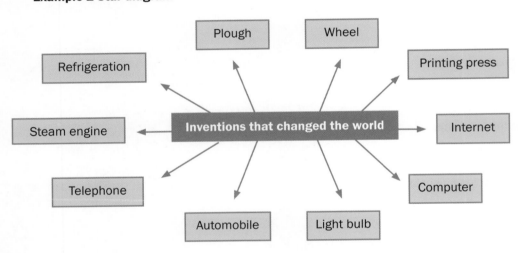

- The central shape such as a circle or a rectangle has the topic.
- Radiating out from it to make a star design are ideas or facts about the topic.

Example 3 Venn diagram

- Named after its designer, John Venn.
- Shows relationships by overlapping shapes, usually circles.
- Shows data that applies to just one element, such as Sparta OR Athens.
- Shows data that applies to both elements, such as Sparta AND Athens.

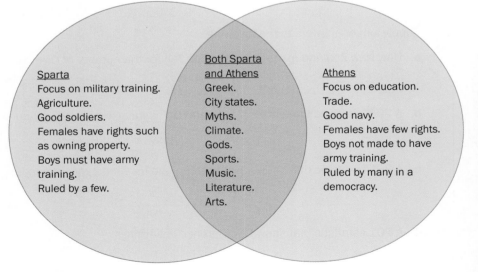

 ISBN: 9780170389334

Example 4 Fishbone or Ishikawa diagram

- Also called Ishikawa diagram after its designer, Kaoru Ishikawa.
- A way to show an important historical idea – that historical change takes place through the process of cause and effect, which is the process of one thing leading to another, and so on.

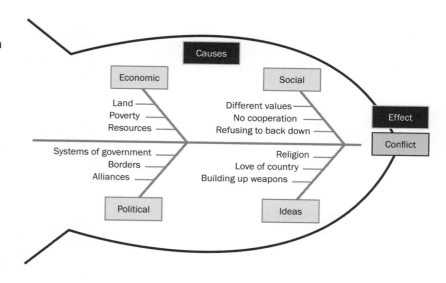

Example 5 Flowchart

- Represents flowing such as a process.
- Shows the stages or steps of the flow in boxes joined together with arrows.
- The steps flow in order, with the first step leading to the second, the second step leading to the third, and so on.

George Washington becomes President

Born 1732 into a planter family in Virginia which was, like the other colonies in the US, ruled by Britain.

↓

He disliked British interference in his business.

↓

He was elected Commander in Chief of the Continental Army (army of British colonies in US).

↓

From 1775 to 1783 he led troops in war against Britain, which US won.

↓

In 1787 he was elected the first President of the US.

1 Put the data provided into the shape to make a pyramid diagram.

DATA Soldiers and scribes, Slaves, High government officials, Social classes in Ancient Egypt, Lower government officials, Pharaoh, Farmers and unskilled workers

2 Say what sort of diagram would best fit the following.

a Results of the Second World War. _____

b Differences and similarities of Ancient Rome and Ancient Greece. _____

c The social structure of medieval England. _____

d Causes of the Syrian Civil War. _____

e How the discovery of penicillin was a happy accident. _____

Interpreting tables

Table = a way to arrange historical data in rows and columns.

Example 1

Unemployed in NZ Depression

Year	Number
1929	2,897
1930	5,318
1931	41,431
1932	51,549
1933	46,944
1934	39,235
1935	38,234
1936	36,890

Example 2

Percentage of male/female population in NZ provinces 1871

Province	Males	Females	Excess of males
Auckland	56.95	43.05	13.90
Taranaki	57.41	42.59	14.82
Wellington	54.91	45.09	9.82
Hawke's Bay	59.35	40.65	18.70
Nelson	63.36	36.64	26.72
Marlborough	61.79	38.21	23.58
Canterbury	55.08	44.92	10.16
Westland	68.06	31.94	36.12
Otago	60.56	39.44	21.12
Southland	56.11	43.89	12.22
Average	58.64	41.36	17.28

Example 3

Places of birth for people living In New Zealand 1867

Place	Number
England	65,614
Ireland	27,955
Scotland	34,826
Wales	1319
New Zealand	64,052
Australian colonies	11,313
Other British Dominions	3798
United States of America	1213
France	553
Germany	2838
Other foreign countries (including China)	3667
At sea	751
Not specified	769
TOTAL	**218,668**

Example 4

2012 New Zealanders connected to the internet

Age	Percentage
15–24	93
25–34	94
35–44	91
45–54	85
55–64	77
65–74	61
75+	32

Example 5

2012 New Zealanders' online entertainment

Activity	Percentage
Games	26
Music	49
Movies, images	47
Books, news	42
TV, radio	37

ISBN: 9780170389334

Example 6

Top social media sites August 2013 New Zealand

Type	Number	Percentage
YouTube	2,460,430	59.91
Facebook	2,400,000	53.56
WordPress	1,020,238	22.77
Tumblr	757,707	16.91
Linkedin	697,028	15.56
Twitter	368,036	8.21
Pinterest	252,797	5.64
Instagram	218,140	4.87

Type	Number	Percentage
TripAdvisor	165,296	3.69
Flickr	144,033	3.21
MySpace	74,815	1.67
Foursquare	30,850	0.69
Stumbleupon	27,769	0.62
Reddit	16,052	0.36
Bebo	6604	0.15

1 Answer the following question.

Statistics New Zealand gives you links to census subjects in NZ.Stat, which is an online tool that lets you build your own tables. Say how that would be useful to you as a historian.

_____

_____

_____

2 Give the number/s of the table examples you would use if you were researching the following about New Zealand.

a Where 19th century immigrants came from.

_____

b The results of an event in the 1930s.

_____

c The history of leisure internet use.

_____

d Changing ratios of the sexes.

_____

3 Provide the following data from the tables.

a The total population in 1867. _____

b The date of greatest unemployment in the Great Depression. _____

c The most popular online entertainment in 2012. _____

d The number of people in 1867 who had been born in England. _____

e The number of people in 1867 who had been born in New Zealand. _____

f The top three social media sites in August 2013. _____

Recognising graphs

Graphs = diagrams that show a relationship by using a symbol such as a curve, a series of bars or a line.

Example 1 Line graph

- *y*-axis shows population in thousands.
- *x*-axis shows date in years.
- Two lines of two different colours show Maori population and Pakeha population.

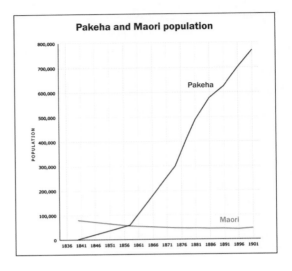

Example 2 Pie graph

- Called a pie graph because of its shape.
- The whole pie adds up to 100 percent.
- Slices or segments of the pie show percentages of 100, such as 25%.

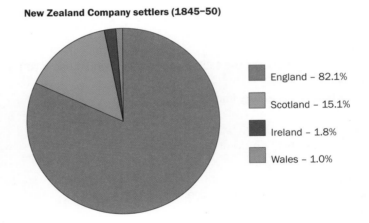

Example 3 Pictograph (or pictogram)

- Pictures or images show data.
- Each single item of the picture or image stands for a certain number of things.

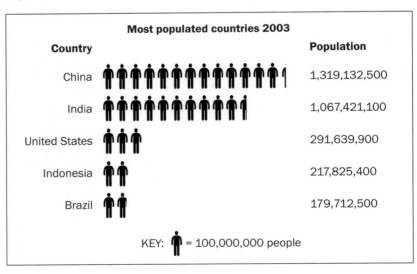

   ISBN: 9780170389334

Example 4 Bar graph

- Shows data by using rectangular bars.
- Bars run horizontally.
- Bars are of equal width.
- Spaces between bars are equal.
- Has a title.
- *y*-axis shows years of elections.
- *x*-axis shows numbers of MPs (Members of Parliament).

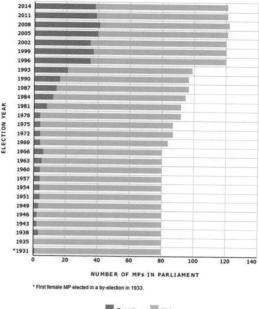

Female and male MPs in New Zealand 1931–2014

* First female MP elected in a by-election in 1933.

Female   Male

Example 5 Column graph

- Bars are vertical, like columns, so called a column graph.
- Has a title.
- Bars are equal width.
- Spaces between bars are equal.
- *y*-axis shows tonnes of carbon dioxide equivalent.
- *x*-axis shows countries.

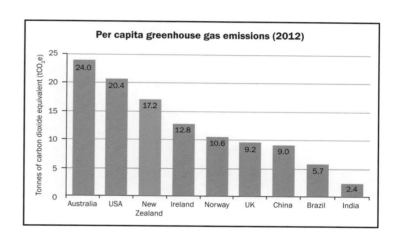

Example 6 Histogram

- Graphical display of data using bars and grouping numbers into groups, which is why the population pyramid shown here is an example of a histogram.
- Made up of two back-to-back horizontal histograms.
- One is for males and one is for females.

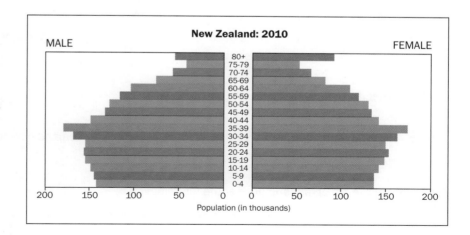

1 Look at the line graph and answer the following.

a   Why is it called a line graph? _____

b   What is the title of the graph? _____

c   In what year did Pakeha population reach the Maori population? _____

d   Why does the y-axis go up 800,000? _____

e   What happens to the Pakeha population? _____

f   What happens to the Maori population? _____

2 Look at the pie graph and answer the following.

a   Why is it called a pie graph? _____

b   What do the percentages of the slices add up to? _____

c   What is the link between the graph and New Zealand? _____

3 Look at the pictograph and answer the following.

a   Where do you find what the symbol stands for? _____

b   Say if you think the symbol helps or does not help to explain the population numbers.

_____

4 Look at the bar graph and answer the following.

a   Why is the graph called a bar graph?

_____

b   Why are there two colours?

_____

c   How many MPs were there in 1966? _____

d   Make a comment about the comparison between numbers of female and male MPs during the entire period of the graph.

_____

5 Look at the column graph and answer the following.

a   Carbon dioxide equivalent is used to describe different greenhouse gases in a common unit. What is its abbreviation?

_____

b   What does emissions mean?

_____

c   Which three countries' combined total is closest to New Zealand's per capita emission?

_____

6 Look at the histogram and answer the following.

a   Give a reason why a population pyramid is a histogram.

_____

b   What do the numbers in the middle, starting at 0-4, represent?

_____

c   What happens to the ratios between male and female towards the top of the histogram?

_____

From 1853 to 1976, New Zealand was divided into provinces.

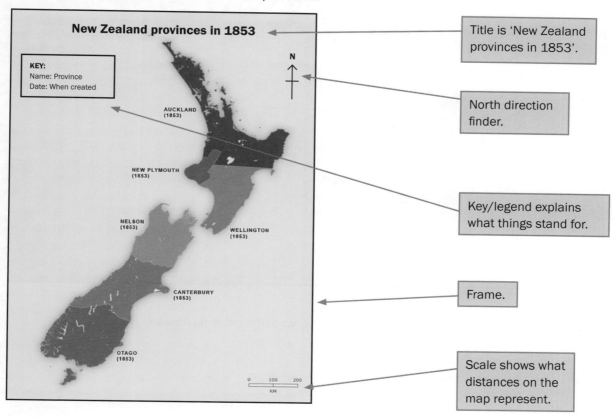

New Zealand provinces in 1853

KEY:
Name: Province
Date: When created

AUCKLAND
(1853)

NEW PLYMOUTH
(1853)

NELSON
(1853)

WELLINGTON
(1853)

CANTERBURY
(1853)

OTAGO
(1853)

N

0   100   200
KM

Title is 'New Zealand provinces in 1853'.

North direction finder.

Key/legend explains what things stand for.

Frame.

Scale shows what distances on the map represent.

1

New Zealanders on board a troopship on the way to Britain on 21 April 1941 during World War Two being taught how to read maps. Soldiers were going to fight in foreign countries and basic mapping skills could mean the difference between life and death.

Explain why these Kiwi soldiers were lucky to get a lesson in map skills.

_____

_____

2

Name some features that could have improved this hand-drawn map of Syria and the direction in which people fled.

_____

_____

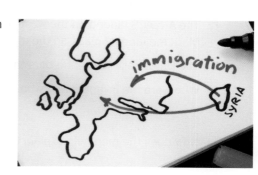

The unrest that erupted into civil war in Syria began in 2011 and caused many to flee the country.

"THE GRAPHIC" MAP OF THE DARDANELLES OPERATIONS 1915

Karachali, the scene of the landing of British troops on August 7.

3 Look at the map of the Dardanelles (above) and answer the following about it.

a Why is the map a primary source? _____

b What, apart from its date, suggests it is a very old map? _____

c Name a helpful feature the map has and name a helpful feature it does not have.

_____

d A natural feature on maps is made by nature. Name one on this map. _____

e A cultural feature on maps is made by people. Name one on this map. _____

f In which direction does the rest of Turkey lie? _____

g What does it suggest about the terrain (landscape)? _____

h A peninsula is a piece of land projecting out into a body of water. How does Gallipoli qualify to be called a

peninsula? _____

i The Dardanelles is a narrow strait that separates European Turkey from Asian Turkey. The Gallipoli peninsula is in European Turkey. Write on the map the location of the Dardanelles.

j The ANZACS landed on the west side of the peninsula about opposite to where the peninsula narrows. Mark the landing place on the map.

k The Dardanelles Strait borders the southwest of the Aegean Sea. Mark this sea on the map.

l Who were the invaders and who were the defenders in 1915?

_____

m How does the map help explain why the invading forces did not manage to win the battle for Gallipoli?

_____

 ISBN: 9780170389334

Captions = titles or brief explanations for an image such as a photograph.

The image aims to provide an emotional reaction from the viewer.

The caption helps explain the why, where, who, what, when and how.

Just hours after this photo of the Hindenburg over New York City on May 6 1937 was taken, the airship crashes and burns while trying to land at Lakehurst in New Jersey.

Tips for creating captions

- Use present tense to describe events in the image. *Edmund Hillary stands at the top of the world in 1953.*
- Give information that the reader can't get just from looking at the image. *Two minutes later, the tsunami sweeps the man away.*
- Don't use unnecessary words such as 'above' or 'here' or 'is pictured'. *Immigrants from Syria come ashore.*
- Don't start with words such as 'A', 'An', 'The'. *Unidentified woman saves baby in flood.*
- Label images correctly, such as the year the photo was taken. *Russian dog in 1957 is first animal to orbit Earth.*
- Avoid being judgemental or critical. *Lee Harvey Oswald, who assassinated President Kennedy in 1963.*
- Identify when photos have been digitally improved. *Colour tinting brings 1840 mission house in Northland back to life.*
- Don't try to be funny if the image is not. *Scientists say they have found even older examples of the extinct small human species* Homo floresiensis, *dubbed the Hobbit.*
- Don't try to decide how a person is feeling. *New Zealander Anthony Wilding after his fourth Wimbledon Singles title victory.*
- Avoid descriptive terms such as 'beautiful' or 'dreadful' even when the image shows this. *Australia's Chappell bowls underarm to New Zealand's McKechnie in 1981 international cricket match.*

1 Rewrite the following captions to improve them.

   a Serbian Novak Djokovic had huge grin plastered on his face after beating grumpy Scot to win Roland Garros tennis title.

   _____

   _____

   b The doll that an Indonesian fisherman found on a beach and stupidly thought was an angel that fell from the sky. People will believe anything!

   _____

   _____

2 For each of the four images below, create a suitable caption.

a _____

_____

b _____

_____

c _____

_____

d _____

_____

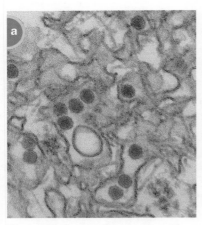

Clue = Zika fever outbreak, caused by mosquito-borne virus and which can cause birth defects, began in April 2015 in Brazil, and spread to other American countries.

Clue = Chariot racing was popular in Ancient Rome and Ancient Greece and a sport that females were allowed to watch, whereas they were banned from watching many others. Because the chariots were light and collisions happened, a driver might be killed or badly injured.

Clue = Samuel Marsden's first service in New Zealand, at Oihi Bay, Rangihoua, Bay of Islands; his translator, Ruatara, is on his right, and his brig *Active* is moored in the stream.

Clue = Apollo 11 was the first lunar landing mission with a crew of three astronauts, two of whom set foot on the moon's surface on July 20 in 1969.

 ISBN: 9780170389334

Tiriti o Waitangi Treaty of Waitangi	**Taonga** treasure, natural resource such as river or cultural resource such as an artefact
Whenua land	**Waiata** song, chant
Tapu sacred, special, not ordinary; when tapu is removed, things become **noa**	**Moko** tattoo
Hui meeting, conference	**Whanau** extended family
Kingitanga Maori King Movement	**Tamariki** children
Marae area for formalities in front of meeting house or whole complex including meeting house and other features	**Kaumatua** elder/s
	Tikanga Maori customs, traditions, culture
Tangata whenua original people belonging to a place	**Koha** acknowledging hospitality with a gift, food or money
Kaitiakitanga guardianship, protection, caring for the environment	**Korero purakau** legend, myth, story; explains action or event
Pakeha people living in NZ of English/European origin; recently often used for any non-Maori	**Tangihanga** ceremony for mourning deceased person
	Mana authority, honour, respect, power
Tino rangatiratanga self-determination, chiefly authority, rights and responsibilities to do with managing and controlling resources	**Turangawaewae** place to stand or belong
	Ururupa grave, cemetery
Whakapapa genealogy (ancestry line)	**Mana whenua** customary right or authority held by group such as iwi in particular area
Karakia prayers, words for a special purpose	**Tangata** people
Manaakitanga welcoming and looking after guests	**Manuhiri** guests
Rangatira chiefly rank	**Te Reo Maori** language
Haka chant with dance	**Mihi** formal way of respecting by acknowledging and greeting people
Iwi tribe, has boundaries within which it has mana whenua; standing	**Waka** canoe
Hapu clan, sub-tribe	**Raupatu** confiscate, take by force
Rohe boundary	**Tipuna** ancestors

1 Find the Maori term that best fits the following.

a Signed in 1840 when NZ became a British colony _____

b Group smaller than an iwi _____

c Physical place important to iwi _____

d Legend of how the Kiwi lost its wings _____

e Place of burial _____

f History of your family ancestors _____

g Being sustainable and making sure resources are available for future generations

_____

h Prized possession such as a greenstone club _____

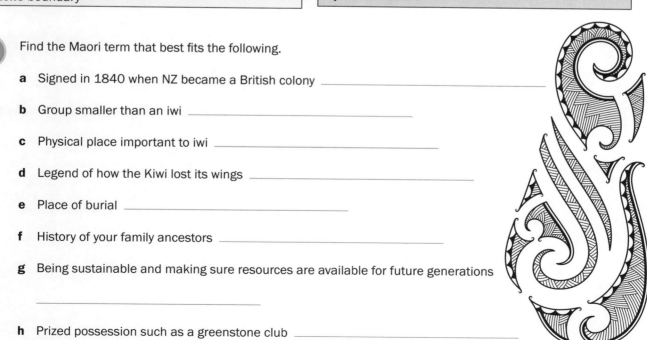

i What Polynesians used to get to New Zealand _____

j Title of rank _____

k What Maori would have called land confiscation by the Government after the NZ Wars

_____

l This group sang as soldiers invaded Parihaka Pa in 1881 and adults offered no resistance

_____

m A social gathering or assembly _____

n Maori are said to be this in New Zealand _____

o Social group smaller than a hapu _____

p The Maori way of doing things _____

q Historically associated with battles, today used by groups such as All Blacks

_____

r A woman might have one on her mouth and chin as a sign of mana

_____

s Its headquarters were at Turangawaewae Marae at Ngaruawahia in the Waikato

_____

t Might be said in order to increase the likelihood of a good result _____

2 List the first six and the last six terms that would appear if the terms were arranged in an alphabetical glossary.

_____

_____

_____

3 Make a comment about why people in other countries are becoming increasingly interested in the history of Maori.

_____

_____

_____

_____

_____

_____

  ISBN: 9780170389334

How to answer multi-choice questions on a source

These can test how well you understand a topic by giving you a source and asking you a question with several answers and you have to choose the best answer.

Examples

Source 1

This space station belongs to a family of spacecraft that began their existence in the same year as

a) New Zealand's Upper House of Parliament ceased to exist in 1951

b) the inauguration of Egypt's Aswan High Dam in 1971

c) Germany voted to shift its capital from Bonn to Berlin in 1991.

The answer is **b)**. If you were studying the history of space exploration you would know that the first space station was Salyut 1, which the Soviet Union launched in 1971.

Mir above New Zealand.

Source 2

The most likely setting for the people in the drawing, Sun King Louis XIV and a noblewoman, would be

a) Paris in the French Revolution

b) Marseilles in the Allied liberation

c) Versailles in the 17th century.

The answer is **c)**. If you were studying French history you would know that the Revolution started in 1789, long after the death of Louis XIV, that the Allies liberated Marseilles from the Germans in 1944, and that Louis XIV made Versailles the centre of his political power.

1 Look at the source and answer the question.

This set of elements most likely symbolises

a) Ancient Egypt

b) Ancient Rome

c) Ancient Greece.

2 Look at the source and answer the question.

The correct statement about the named countries is that

a) the majority are in Europe

b) the majority are in North America

c) the majority are in the Pacific and Asia.

Top 10 for resettling refugees 2014	
(per million of country's population)	
Australia	516
Canada	360
Norway	263
USA	234
Sweden	210
Finland	203
NZ	169
Liechtenstein	139
Denmark	62
Luxembourg	55

3 Look at the source and answer the question.

The wall splitting it into two came down in 1989 but this historical sign to show how the country was divided into zones remains in the city of

a) Moscow

b) Berlin

c) Paris.

4 The German who emigrated to the United States in 1933 with his wife after the Nazis targeted them for being Jewish, and who went on to win the Nobel Prize for Physics, was

a) Rudolph Valentino

b) Ernest Rutherford

c) Albert Einstein.

 ISBN: 9780170389334

Short answer questions can test how well you understand a topic by giving you a source and asking you questions about it that have only one totally correct answer.

Short answers can test how well you interpret or understand a source by asking you to find evidence.

Example

1 What is the name of the country?
2 What is the name of the strait?
3 What are the most southern and most northern named points?
4 Which name was added after 25 April 1915?

Example

Give two pieces of evidence that show this is an American poster.

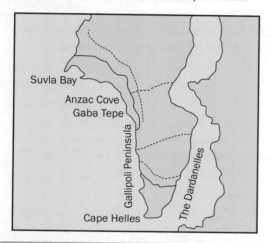

1 Turkey, 2 Dardanelles, 3 Cape Helles, Suvla Bay, 4 Anzac Cove.

The man pointing is Uncle Sam, who represents the US, and he is holding the US flag.

1

a Name the mountain range.

b Name the country.

c Name the two men who climbed the named mountain first.

d What does B.C. stand for?

2

a Name the civilisation.

b Name the ruler.

c Name the profession that used the objects.

d Name the pronged weapon.

21 | How to make sure you answer the question

All you have to do is to READ the question and then ANSWER it. One of the skills you are being tested on is how well you can follow directions.

The question said '*Give one piece of evidence that shows ...*' and Kev spent a lot of time writing about two pieces of evidence. The marker looked only at the first piece but Kev had got that wrong. No marks.

The question said '*Give the approximate distance Alexander's army went.*' Jeni worked out a distance with several decimal points in it. No extra marks and a rush to finish the rest of the questions.

The question said '*Refer to Source B.*' Von decided to use Source C instead because she understood it better. No marks.

The question said '*Quote the sentence from the first paragraph that is an opinion.*' Alice thought the sentence was too long and rewrote it in her own words. No quote, no marks.

The question asked for the essay length to be about a page. Raz loved the topic and wrote five pages but his first page was just the introduction. Low mark, line put through last four pages by marker.

 ISBN: 9780170389334

The question was an essay about why the policy of apartheid started in South Africa. Jac did not like the idea of apartheid and most of her essay was about how bad it was. Low mark.

_____

_____

The question was about imagining you were the Prime Minister giving a speech about historic links with partners in a proposed trade deal. Piri was a fan of the PM and so he listed all the achievements of his government and mentioned the historic links only in passing. Low mark.

_____

_____

1 In the space provided, put what each student should have done to get a better mark.

2 Give advice that would help this student answer the questions in the exam.

How to use right writing

To make sure you have prepared your material the best you can and to qualify for excellent grades, you need to use right writing.

1 Read the question carefully and do not go off task. Not The answer to 'Who are the people?' is King Tutankhamen, a pharaoh of Ancient Egypt, and his half-sister and wife, and I'd also like to add that I've got a good theory on how he died, which I'll now explain but …

_____

_____

2 Use capitals for titles, places and sentence beginnings, and full stops for sentence endings. Not king tutankhamen came from ancient egypt but …

_____

_____

3 Avoid slang. Not The dude was a weirdo who ruled only from about the age of ten to nineteen but the world thinks his death-mask is cool but …

_____

_____

4 Avoid silly sentences. Not Discovering King Tut's tomb in 1922 people said Howard Carter died of the so-called curse of the pharaohs (**People did not discover the tomb; Howard Carter did**) but …

_____

_____

5 Avoid 'etc.' as it suggests you have run out of ideas. Not This battle blocked some French forces reaching Waterloo and so helped the British etc. defeat Napoleon but …

_____

_____

6 Keep tenses the same. Not The battles of Wavre and Waterloo took place on the same day and mean the French lose the Napoleonic Wars but …

_____

_____

7 Be tidy. If a marker cannot read it, you cannot get marks. Not The battles of Wavre and Waterloo took place on the same day but …

_____

_____

8 Watch apostrophes. Not Napoleons' horses but …

_____

_____

9 Avoid contractions. Not Germans couldn't believe how black athlete Jesse Owens spoiled their party but ...

_____

_____

_____

10 Watch _there_ and _their_. Not there party but ...

_____

11 Avoid abbreviations. Not J Lovelock from NZ won gold at the B Olympics but ...

_____

_____

12 Watch its and it's. Not Germany used it's Olympics for propaganda, and Hitler said things like 'Its good for Nazism' but ...

_____

_____

1 In the blank places in the 12 points above, write the correct versions.

2 Circle the mistakes made in this comment about the old poster.

> the ussr doesn't exist The union breaks up in 1991 it was countries like russia etc It's hammer and sickle are the unions' symbols

Then put a correct version in the box below.

How to create a paragraph

Paragraph = a group of sentences with a common topic and starting a new line in a piece of writing.

Example

1 Topic sentence introduces the main idea.

2 Supporting details give facts, examples, explanations.

3 Closing sentence restates the main idea.

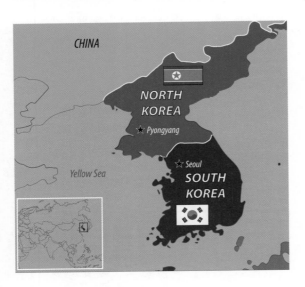

The Korean War began in 1950 when soldiers from the communist-backed Democratic People's Republic of Korea in the north invaded the pro-Western Republic of Korea in the south. The United Nations asked the invading force to leave the south and when this did not happen, it gathered an army to defend the south. New Zealand, which was worried that communism was starting to spread through Asia, joined 15 other countries in a war in Korea against the communists. The Korean War ended in 1953 and Korea is still divided into North Korea and South Korea.

1 Draw an arrow from each of the three points in the example on the left to one of the colour blocks of text on the right to show how they match up.

2 Rearrange the following to make a logical paragraph.
a The final vote
b being too much like the Australian flag
c resulted in the old flag being kept.
d and arguments against change included it being the one
e In 2015-6 New Zealanders were able to vote on
f Kiwis fought and died under.
g Arguments for change included the Union Jack flag
h changing the national flag.

How to create a history essay

> History essay = a piece of non-fiction made up of paragraphs on a particular subject.

Example

If you had to create an essay about an invention of Thomas Edison, you could choose his favourite, the 1877 phonograph. Points to mention could include how he worked out the secret to recording sound, his first message, his amazed reaction when he heard his machine play it back to him, his suggestions for uses of the phonograph, and other uses he had not thought of such as soldiers being able to take music to war to cheer themselves up.

> Structure of an essay = how it is created and what parts it has. Having a structure for an essay makes it easier to create, to read and to mark. This helps you to research (find information), organise (put information in order), outline (make paragraph headings), write, and edit (proofread).

Head = introduction, what the essay is about.

Tail = summary of the main ideas.

Body = several paragraphs, each one about a different idea.

1 List five history topics you might be interested in creating an essay about.

_____

_____

_____

2 State what the image has to do with writing a history paragraph.

_____

_____

_____

_____

3 State why it is useful to have a mental picture of an animal when planning the structure of a history essay.

_____

_____

How to show quotations

Quotations = quotes, words presented from a source such as a person or book exactly as they appeared. For example, a famous French historian called Alphonse de Lamartine said, '*History teaches us everything, even the future.*'

'*We shall fight on the beaches, we shall fight on the landing grounds, we shall fight in the fields and in the streets ...; we shall never surrender.*'

'*Veni, vidi, vici.*' [I came, I saw, I conquered.]

Guidelines

1. Put the quotation inside quotation marks, single or double ones. The rules for single or double depend on which country you are in.
2. If you use single quotation marks for quotations, use double ones to show a quotation within the quotation, and vice versa.
3. Put the punctuation mark, such as a full stop, that ends the quotation inside the quotation mark.
4. If you do not use all the words of the quotation, put three dots (called an ellipsis) to show this.
5. Put anything you add in square brackets.
6. For long quotes, indent the quotes and omit quotation marks.

'*There is a homely adage which runs: "Speak softly and carry a big stick."*'

William Sherman, who was a General in the Union Army during the American Civil War, gave a speech to some of his former troops, saying:

> *There is many a boy here today who looks on war as all glory, but, boys, it is all hell. You can bear this warning voice to generations yet to come. I look upon war with horror.*

1 Draw arrows from the six guidelines to examples.

2 Add the missing quotation marks to the following.

In February 2016 Pope Francis went to the border between the US and Mexico where he criticised leaders on both sides. The 'forced migration' of thousands of Central Americans was, he said, a human tragedy. Being faced with so many legal vacuums, the Pope said, they get caught up in a web that ensnares and always destroys the poorest. He spoke against immigration policies that push people into the hands of drug gangs and human smugglers. We cannot deny the humanitarian crisis, the Pope said. Each step, a journey laden with grave injustices: the enslaved, the imprisoned and extorted; so many of these brothers and sisters of ours are the consequence of trafficking in human beings.

 ISBN: 9780170389334

> Bibliography = a list of sources such as books and the web that you used to write an essay outside an exam.

Use a bibliography

- to show you are not trying to pass someone's work off as your own original work (that is known as plagiarism)
- to show how widely you researched your topic
- to show you did not just make up key facts and quotations
- to give readers sources for extra information if they want to do more research on the topic.

General guide for a simple bibliography

- Book = author (last name first), title, city of publication, publisher, year of publication, e.g. Yan T., *Humans in Space*, London, Orbit, 2016.
- Web = author, address, item's name, date, e.g. Wikipedia, https://en.wikipedia.org/wiki/Space_exploration, Space Exploration, 26 April 2016.
- Encyclopaedia = encyclopaedia title, edition date, volume number, title of article, page numbers, e.g. *New Knowledge Library*, 1981, Vol. 28, Space Travel and Exploration, pp. 2652–56.
- Magazine = author, title of article, name of magazine, volume number/date, page numbers, e.g. L. Sing, Space Travel, *Voyager*, Vol. 5, February 2014, pp. 1–5.
- Newspaper = author, title of article, name of newspaper, city, date, section, page number/s e.g. J. Martine, Upwards, *Gazette*, Wenbridge, 3 April 2016, World section, p. 9.
- Person = name, occupation, date of interview, e.g. Pran, W., lecturer, 12 January 2016.
- Film = title, director, distributor, year, e.g. *The Martian*, Ridley Scott, 20th Century Fox, 2015.
- Email = author, date, subject, available address, e.g. NASA, 2016, Space exploration, Contact NASA.

1   Highlight any of the above sources you have used to find information on a topic you have studied in class.

2   Suggest types of sources that a student could consult for an essay about the Christchurch earthquakes and that she could use in a bibliography.

_____

_____

_____

_____

_____

_____

_____

How to make a glossary

Glossary = a list of technical or more difficult terms used in a source, along with their meanings, usually appearing at the end of the source.

Example

If you had prepared a history of robotics, your glossary might include these terms.

AIBO entertainment robot designed by Sony

Artificial intelligence capability of machine to imitate human behaviour

Automated functioning without continuous input

Autonomous without pre-programmed behaviours and human supervision

Cloud robotics robots given more intelligence and capacity from cloud

Cyborg person with mechanical or electrical devices

Data glove input device for human-computer interaction

Dynamics study of forces that cause motion

Grey goo scenario if self-replicating robots got out of control

Microrobot machine maybe only fraction of millimetre in size

Pressure sensing allows robot to measure and know force

Robot machine able to do task/s repeatedly with speed and precision

Robotics branch of engineering to do with robots

Workspace maximum points robot can reach

1 State four things about how the glossary is set out.

a _____

b _____

c _____

d _____

2 Add the following terms to the glossary to show where they should go. Add any meanings you know.

Locomotion, Vision sensor, Flexibility, Laser, Integrate, Gripper, Error, Debug, Controller, Manipulator.

3 Give two terms and meanings for a glossary if you had prepared a history of your favourite sport or music.

_____

_____

Example

The text in the orange box below was posted on the net as a happy story. Many accepted the story as true and it flew around the world. However, many more discerning people pointed out some facts (in the blue boxes).

> Discerning = being able to make good judgements such as deciding whether a source is likely to be correct or not.

Alexander was seven years younger than Winston and probably too small to rescue him.

Winston did get ill with what was probably pneumonia but he was not treated with penicillin for it.

Winston was unlikely to have been in the isolated part of Scotland where the Flemings lived.

A poor Scottish farm lad called Alexander Fleming saved a young man called Winston Churchill from drowning. Winston's father was so grateful that he paid for Alexander to be educated and become the doctor he had dreamed of being. Alexander became Sir Alexander, famous discoverer of penicillin. Winston became Sir Winston, famous British Prime Minister. When Winston lay ill with pneumonia, penicillin saved him.

There was another version of the story that said it was Alexander's father who had saved Winston.

Alexander did not leave the farm to race off to medical school but did other jobs first.

Alexander's medical education was paid for by an inheritance from an uncle.

No biographer has found evidence of the story.

1 What had the more discerning people done that people who believed the Fleming-Churchill story had not done?

_____

_____

2 Underline evidence that discerning people produced.

3 Highlight or underline the skills in the box that would help you be a discerning historian.

searching for the truth	focusing on one source such as Wikipedia
defending your opinion regardless of evidence	looking for evidence
keeping an open mind	willing to accept without questions
willing to change opinions	using a wide variety of sources

How to use evidence

Evidence = something that helps prove or disprove a story or statement. For example: If a couple denied they had had a relationship, a photograph would provide evidence of lying.

You can collect and present evidence. Mai found a copy of her great-grandfather's birth certificate, which she used as <u>evidence</u> he was born in Bulgaria.

You can examine sources to find evidence to prove a statement. Tess found <u>evidence</u> in three tables of trade figures that gold was an important New Zealand export in the 1860s.

You can use any type of source as evidence. Jules collected copies of three cartoons about the 1981 Springbok rugby tour of New Zealand as <u>evidence</u> of how deeply it affected society. Assi produced his father's diary and a photo of his bombed house as <u>evidence</u> he was a Syrian refugee. Stig collected a copy of the original plans for the local community as <u>evidence</u> for how much the area had changed. The British Museum's *A History of the World in 100 Objects* included <u>evidence</u> such as an early Victorian tea set, a Roman British pot, a mummy, a jade axe, an early writing tablet, the Rosetta Stone, clay model of cattle and a credit card.

1 Give two examples of digital evidence.

_____

_____

_____

_____

2 A myth is a traditional story that often involves the supernatural and ideas that cannot be proved, while a fact is true. Say why this would be a useful image for your paragraph about historical facts and myths.

_____

_____

_____

3 For what might the following be evidence?

a rock drawing _____

b monument _____

c graffiti on a wall _____

 ISBN: 9780170389334

Answers (can be removed from the centre of the book)

1   Understanding what history means

1   Herodotus lived in ancient times, Greek, wrote first known history, Father of History, no modern technology to help him

2   is about questions, asking questions, finding answers and solutions; this is what history is about and what history students do

2   Understanding what historical information is

1   knowledge through research and inquiry, historical ideas understood after facts have been discovered

3   eg. English transported convicts to Australia, person could become convict for trying to steal bread, there were starving people in England, England used to rule Ireland, Ireland used to be united, English tried to de-Irish the Irish, Irish resisted English efforts, a punishment was pitch-capping

3   Understanding where history happens

1   that time is now in past and what happened can not be undone

2   USA (N America); UK (union of Great Britain [England, Wales, Scotland] and Northern Ireland); France (European mainland close to UK); Russia (NE Europe); Japan (off coast of South Korea); NZ (South Pacific); India (S Asian mainland); Suez Canal (Egypt in N Africa; South Pole (Antarctica); South Africa (southern Africa); Brazil (S America); Gallipoli (peninsula on European part of Turkey)

3   location often helps to explain events and people

4   Understanding social history

2   net has many examples

5   Knowing the 5 Ws and H of history

2   WHY = swept away thousands .., WHAT = tsunami, WHERE = island near ..., WHO = 13-year-old ..., WHEN = Boxing Day and two days, HOW = Because she knew ...

3   When, Where, Who

6   Understanding oral history

2   **a** others interested in listening to their history, **b** giving eye-witness perspective, **c** people may lie to make themselves feel important or interesting

3   eg. **a** family member, doctor, midwife, **b** survivor, person who followed news and/or kept records about it

8   How to create oral history

1   (most involve being impolite, disrespectful, disorganised) eg. **a** 3,4, **b** 1, **c** 2,3,4, **d** 2, **e** 4, **f** 4,6,7, **g** 2, **h** 3,4,5,7

2   involves speaking, usually recorded

9   Knowing about artefacts

1   **a** hair drier, **b** calculator, **c** iron, **d** pencil sharpener, **e** manual meat grinder, **f** diving helmet

10   Understanding what sources are

1   1 museum, 2 postcard, 3 newspaper, 4 camera and phone photos, 5 cemetery, 6 library and books, 7 people's knowledge

11   Knowing the difference between primary and secondary sources

1   **a** S, **b** P, **c** P, **d** S

2   **a** P, **b** S, **c** S, **d** P, **e** S, **f** P

12   Understanding what statistics are

1   before machines, people compiled statistics by hand - time-consuming and laborious; technology reduced risk of human error, meant statistics on wide array of topics accessible on net

2   **a** Tatauranga Aotearoa, **b** every 5 years, **c** 1851, **d** punch cards, **e** 4242048

3   **a** used data based on medals per one million population, **b** 32% of male secondary school students played games for 3 or more hours each day compared with 9% of females, **c** 10% of students met recommendations of 60 minutes of physical activity daily, **d** If NZ was a village of 100 people, 4 earned $100,001 or more, and 38 earned $30000 and less, **e** If NZ was a village of 100 people, 49 people were male and 51 were female

13   Using diagrams

1   title = Social Classes in Ancient Egypt; from top, Pharaoh, High government officials, Lower government officials, Soldiers and scribes, Farmers and unskilled workers, Slaves

2   **a** star, **b** Venn, **c** pyramid, fishbone, **e** flowchart

14   Interpreting tables

1   gives instant access to statistics, allows for creation of tables to suit specific purposes

2   **a** 3, **b** 1, **c** 5,6, **d** 2

3   **a** 218668, **b** 1932, **c** Music, **d** 65614, **e** 64052, **f** YouTube, Facebook, WordPress

15   Recognising graphs

1   **a** lines show changes of population, **b** Pakeha and Maori Population, **c** 1858, **d** by 1901 Pakeha population had reached 770,000, **e** rises dramatically, especially after 1858, **f** declines slowly

2   **a** round shape of pie, **b** 100, **c** shows British settlers who came to NZ with NZ Company

3   **a** key at bottom

4   **a** bars run horizontally, **b** female, male, **c** 120, **d** at no time does number of female MPs get near half number of males

5   **a** tCO2e, **b** amount of greenhouse gas released into atmosphere, **c** China, Brazil, India

6   **a** graphical display of data using bars and grouping numbers into groups, **b** ages, **c** become more unbalanced with female bars longer

16   Understanding historical maps

1   map skills could be vital for survival and not every army provided its soldiers with skills

2   direction finder, title, frame, key (hand-drawn map would not be expected to feature scale)

3   **a** created at time of Dardanelles campaign, **b** looks faded and hand-drawn, lacks computer-generated features, **c** has title, frame; scale, key, direction finder, **d** hills, ocean, **e** ships, **f** east, **g** very hilly, difficult to make progress, **h** long, thin land jutting into Aegean Sea in sw direction, **l** forces such as Anzacs who aimed to capture territory, Turks whose territory it was, **m** shows how defenders had advantage of higher ground

17   How to create captions

1   **a** Serbian Novak Djokovic after defeating Scot to win Roland Garros tennis title, **b** Indonesian fisherman believes doll he finds on beach is angel that fell from sky,

18   Recognising key Maori history terms

1   **a** Tiriti o Waitangi, **b** hapu, whanau, **c** marae, ururupa, **d** korero purakau, **e** ururupa, **f** whakapapa, **g** kaitiakitanga, **h** taonga, **i** waka, **j** rangatira, **k** raupatu, **l** tamariki, **m** hui, **n** tangata whenua, **o** whanau, **p** tikanga Maori, **q** haka, **r** moko, **s** kingitanga, **t** karakia

2   haka, hapu, hui, iwi, kaitiakitanga, karakia; ururupa, whaka, waiata, whanau, whakapapa, whenua

3   increasing understanding and interest in indigenous cultures

19 How to answer multi-choice questions on a source

1 c, **2** a, **3** b, **4** c

20 How to answer short answer questions on a source

1 **a** Himalayas, **b** Nepal, **c** Edmund Hillary, Tenzing Norgay, **d** Base Camp

2 **a** Ancient Rome, **b** Caesar, **c** gladiator, **d** trident

21 How to make sure you answer the question

1 all should have read question properly and followed directions; Kev –one piece of evidence only, Jeni – no decimal points, Von – used Source B, Alice – quoted exact words, Raz – not gone over page limit, Jac – no opinions, Piri –nothing but historic links

2 read question properly, several times if necessary; make sure you understand what answer should be about; make sure everything you write is to do with question

22 How to use right writing

1 **1** The people are King Tutankhamen, a pharaoh of Ancient Egypt, and his half-sister and wife. **2** King Tutankhamen came from Ancient Egypt. **3** Although Tutankhamen ruled only from about the age of ten to nineteen, his death-mask is one of the most famous artefacts in the world. **4** Howard Carter discovered King Tut's tomb in 1922 and when he died, people said he died of the so-called curse of the pharaohs. **5** This battle blocked some French forces reaching Waterloo and so helped the British and their allies defeat Napoleon. **6** The battles of Wavre and Waterloo took place in Belgium. **7** The battles of Wavre and Waterloo took place on the same day. **8** Napoleon's horses. **9** Germans could not believe how black athlete Jesse Owens spoiled their party. **10** their party, **11** Jack Lovelock from New Zealand won gold at the Berlin Olympics. **12** Germany used its Olympics for propaganda, and Hitler said things like 'It's good for Nazism'.

2 the, ussr, doesn't, exist, union, breaks, 1991, Russia, etc, It's, unions' symbols. The USSR does not exist. The Union broke up in 1991. It was countries like Russia. Its hammer and sickle were the Union's symbols.

23 How to create a paragraph

1 In order of appearance.

2 e, h, g, b, d, f, a, c

24 How to create a history essay

2 Research is to find useful information, Organise is to put information in order, Outline is to make paragraph headings, Write is to create essay, Edit is to proofread and make alterations if necessary

3 helps you use basic structure of essay such as introduction, body, conclusion

25 How to show quotations

1 **1** any, or all, **2** 'There is a homely adage ...,' **3** any, or all, **4** 'We shall fight ... ,' **5** Veni, vidi, vici.' **6** William Sherman ...

2 "Being faced with so many legal vacuums," the Pope said, "they get caught up in a web that ensnares and always destroys the poorest." "We cannot deny the humanitarian crisis," the Pope said. "Each step, a journey laden with grave injustices: the enslaved, the imprisoned and extorted; so many of these brothers and sisters of ours are the consequence of trafficking in human beings."

26 How to present a bibliography

2 Book, Web, Magazine, Newspaper, Person, Documentary, TV news item, Email.

27 How to make a glossary

1 **a** alphabetical order, **b** term in bold, **c** meaning is concise, **d** each entry on new line

2 **Locomotion** between Laser and Manipulator = methods robots use to transport themselves from place to place; **Vision sensor** between Robotics and Workspace = identifies object through visual feedback; **Flexibility** between Error and Gray goo = jobs that robot is capable of doing; **Laser** between Integrate and Locomotion = non-contact sensor for robots; **Integrate** between Gripper and Laser = fit together robots with devices; **Gripper** after Gray goo = attached to arm for seizing and holding; **Error** between Dynamics and Flexibility = difference between robot response and order given; **Debug** between Data Glove and Dynamics = interactive device resembling glove; **Controller** between Cloud robotics and Cyborg = usually computer that stores data; **Manipulator** between Locomotion and Microbot = mechanical arm mechanism.

28 How to be discerning

1 thought, found out facts, been discerning

2 all text in 7 blue boxes

3 searching for truth, looking for evidence, keeping open mind, willing to change opinions, using wide variety of sources

29 How to use evidence

1 eg. email, computer printout, digital photo

2 shows facts being stronger than myths by squashing them

3 eg. **a** location and existence of a people, **b** esteem of people for leader, **c** individuals or groups wanting to express themselves in front of public

30 How to use oral historical evidence

1 **a** Seminar, **b** Recorded conversation, **c** Whakapapa, **d** Report, **e** Discussion, **f** Speech, **g** Review

2 for deaf or hard-of-hearing person, for long process where useful to have written copy to refer back to, to have historical written official document for future, as proof that something was said or happened

31 How to use written historical evidence

1 **a** broadside, **b** letter, newspaper, net article, book, log, **c** colour, **d** Votes for women, **e** Internet Of Things, **f** log, official record with periodic entries, **g** somebody wrote it for somebody to read

2 **a** A letter that Glass wrote ..., **b** letter, papers, story, newspapers, journals

32 How to use visual historical evidence

1 **a** j, **b** a, **c** b, **d** d, **e** i, **f** f, **g** e, **h** g, **i** h, **j** c

2 **a** timeline, **b** cartoon, **c** map, **d** photo, **e** diagram, photo, **f** diagram, drawing, **g** painting

33 How to analyse historical cartoons

1 message = brave little Belgium standing up to bullying Germany; Belgium = child armed with thin stick in front of closed gate denying entry, Germany = threatening adult armed with large stick, caption reinforces Belgium's courage

2 message = society has put females in pen by saying their interests should be fashion and gossip rather than politics which is male domain, yet females want to break out of so-called Woman's Sphere, and take part in wider society that includes features like politics; female rejecting toys of fashion and gossip and instead peering over fence into what is closed off to her

3 **a** Brockie, **b** 2 different times, **c** Germany, Russia, **d** Czechoslovakia, Ukraine, **e** wolf, bear, **f** unfriendly, **g** have seized prey, **h** will eat prey

34 How to use performance historical evidence

1 mime, play, waiata, role play, practical demonstration, tableau, concert, Kapa Haka, Symphony Orchestra, Choir, workshop demonstration, dance, Sound and Light show, songs, conch music, Last Post, musical revue

2 **a** practical demonstration, **b** mime, role play, skit, short play, **c** short play, **d** tableau

35 How to use appropriate format and style

1 from left, 3, 2, 1, 4 (2 and 1 interchangeable)

2 appropriate, style, headline, words, paragraph, what, information or details, accounts, tragedy, serious, digital, mobiles.

3 **a** l, **b** l, **c** F, **d** F, **e** F, **f** F, **g** l, **h** F, **i** F, **j** l, **k** F, **l** l

36 How to analyse historical photographs and posters

1 **a** image is poster, soldier in foreground, mother and child in

 ISBN: 9780170389334

middle ground, burning village in background, soldier stands, defiant expression, mother and child fleeing, text at top and bottom, top text dominant as it is larger, red, underlined, **b** Recruitment poster, designed to get men to enlist, published after 4 August 1914 when Germany invaded Belgium, appeals to emotions

2 **a** construction site, worker in foreground, city in background, photo not coloured, skyscrapers, overcast or smog, **b** before 1931, Empire State Building, different safety rules at that time, worker did not suffer from vertigo, photographer also did not suffer from vertigo

37 How to Recognise Setting

1 **a** Jan 4 Colombo's Gemology in Sri Lanka, **b** Jan 5 inter-school match at Kalyan, **c** Jan 6 North Korea, **d** Jan 6 US, **e** Jan 16 International Space Station, **f** Feb 4 Morocco solar plant near Ouarzazate, **g** Feb 23 Awaroa Inlet beach in the Abel Tasman, **h** Feb 29 Belfast, Northern Ireland

2 flat land around rural settlement, buildings, road

38 Recognising historical context

1 woman with mask (Visual), In 2002, SARS (Event), The country's culture of silence (Context); Edge of the world (Visual), Lack of knowledge and technology (Event), Many ancient cultures believed (Context); Witches being bunt at the stake (Visual), Many people in medieval Europe (Event), Human rights and tolerance were centuries (Context); Soldiers on a train (Visual), In 1914 many young men (Event), The pace of life was much slower (Context); African American fugitive running (Visual), In 1955 a black woman (Event), Racial segregation and discrimination (Context)

2 executions carried out in haste and burials in secret, no official records, no DNA testing, revolution produces climate of rumour and guessing, much of population ill-educated and never seen Tsar or his family

3 by 2016 many countries, including New Zealand, had laws about equal rights for females and outlawing discrimination on basis of gender, also International Declaration of Human Rights, women therefore able to vote; 1816 women had no such equality and they were expected to conform to strict social rules such as accepting that politics was male preserve only

39 Understanding perspective

1 **a** education, socio-economic position, work, **b** religion, **c** experience, proximity, eyesight, **d** age, gender, **e** time, **f** culture, religion

2 perspective of child will be different to that of adult, probably more imaginative; perspective of business which person has called is it will keep reassuring customers of their importance no matter how long it takes for business to go proactive, customer's perspective is that business keeps person on hold for so long person's life expires

40 How to get into role

1 **a** Alfred Vanderbilt, **b** editor of a German newspaper, **c** steward, **d** Kapitan-leutnant Schweiger, **e** Kaiser Wilhelm II, **f** survivor, **g** editor of a British newspaper, US President, **h** US President

2 not use modern idioms and sayings, be polite and chivalrous, follow rules of Knight Templars such as not having physical contact with females, act bravely and protect pilgrims

41 Understanding a movement

1 Pro-life, Anti-slavery, Suffrage, Occupy Wall Street, Civil Rights, Young Italy, Kingitanga, Hitler Youth, Muslim League, Temperance, Sons of Liberty, Environmental, Peace, Slow Food, Anti-apartheid, Kotahitanga, Taleban, Hippie, Satyagrapha, Mau

2 people who act as a group, an aim everyone in group wants to work for and achieve, a desired change which group wants to bring about, belief that desired change will make society

better, can create conflict with groups wanting to preserve status quo such as government

42 Understanding a social force

1 **a** communism, **b** sustainability, **c** nationalism, **d** democracy, **e** racism, **f** imperialism, **g** industrialisation, **h** robotics, **i** feminism, **j** terrorism, **k** religion, **l** multiculturalism, **m** extremism, **n** urbanisation, **o** globalisation

2 from left: urbanisation, industrialisation, feminism, globalisation

43 Understanding action

1 robbing rich to give to poor; helping poor; climbing Mount Everest; writing plays; flying planes; battling against being struck deaf, mute and blind when young; nursing sick; fighting for France

2 (virtually whole paragraph), said an aim, took control, trained its fighters, took military equipment, ruined some historical sites, displaced millions, turned them into refugees and migrants, ignored the Declaration of Human Rights, caused other countries to wage war

44 Knowing historical conventions

1 **a** weighing, **b** about 130, **c** 50, **d** 1967, **e** 24, **f** CE (Common Era), **g** imperial e.g. pounds and ounces, **h** 1867, **i** 10, **j** Before the Common Era

2 duel as way of settling argument or insult, tophats, cloaks, away from city streets in remote area, pistol in one hand, assistants called seconds, two men firing at each other at close range

45 How to be relevant

1 features 3 young women, published during World War II (clue is clothes such as short sleeves and casual collars), women 'soldiers without guns' as they contribute to war in non-military roles, doing jobs traditionally reserved for males such as working in factories, dressed for physical and office work

2 The cheetah is sometimes .... Swimming is good for asthmatics ..., This was 40 years after ..., Years later the Reichstag ...

46 How to recognise bias

1 X = a, d, e

2 **a** teachers are professionals, trained to present unbiased assessments, report is official document and must be based on facts, **b** eg. Mother – 'He's from another country so he won't be used to your sense of humour.' Son – 'He's always looking for ways to make me look bad for no reason.'

47 How to recognise ambiguity

1 written work should be clear and instantly accessible to prevent any confusion for reader, if assessor can't understand work it will score low assessment

2 eg. **a** While trying to kill a bee Ben Hur accidentally drove his chariot into a tree, **b** Friar Tuck, who had learnt to ride only three months ago, fell asleep and crashed his horse, **c** After the President watched the chimp perform, the chimp was taken to Queen Street and fed two buckets full of bananas, **d** Sue Smith visited the school and many people attended her lecture on 'Nasty Pests', **e** The Governor-General smashed the champagne against the prow and the crowd cheered as the vessel slid down the runway into the tide, **f** Protestors, who released rats in Parliament, were arrested when they left, **g** A case about porn took centre stage at the Supreme Court.

48 How to distinguish between fact and opinion

1 X = should not have

2 from left, F, O, F, O, F, F, O, F, F, O

49 How to avoid anachronisms

1 men standing are Vikings from Scandinavia, device is trebuchet, siege machine which hurls projectiles at enemies and fortifications, associated with Middle Ages when Vikings had stopped raiding, Vikings specialised in swift raids from boats and would not have dragged round heavy machinery, executive's dress and thought place him in modern times, nothing in cartoon matches up

2 person who resists or does not understand modern technologies and machines that do jobs that people used to do

50 Understanding chronology

1 He fell to the ground and the police captured him.

2 F, J, E, C, A, G, B, H, D, I

51 How to prepare an obituary

1 Full name = Richard John Seddon, Nickname/s = King Dick, Old Leather Lungs, Date of birth = 1845, Place of birth = England, Date of death = 10 June 1906, Place of death = on board, Family still alive = wife, daughters and sons, Job title = Premier, Early life = poor student ..., Stature = large, Belief/s = against Asian immigration ..., stopped Chinese from getting Old-Age Pension, gum-diggers from Dalmatia 'a plague of locusts', 'God's Own Country', Quote/s = 'Then learn him', Formal language = all of obituary, Action/s = made government department hire West Coaster, introduced Old Age Pensions, gave up his cigars, Conventions of the time = see answer to 2.

2 Prime Minister/Premier, Mount Taranaki/Mount Egmont, metres/ feet, kg/stones and pounds

52 How to use a timeline

1 use present tense, chronological order, on any topic, useful way to show data so it is more quickly accessible, different formats and shapes

2 n order: 1977 First Star Wars ..., 1997 IBM computer ..., 2000 ASIMO, 2002 Roomba ..., 2005 First self-replicating robot, 2010 NZ Rex ..., 2013 Kirobo ...

53 How to measure time

1 **a** Renaissance, **b** Hiroshima, Nagasaki, **c** Fall of the Western Roman Empire, **d** Century, **e** Ice Ages, **f** Prehistory, **g** Sputnik 1, **h** The Age of Discovery, **i** The Elizabethan Age, **j** term The Dark Ages, **k** Napoleonic Era, **l** The Golden Age of Piracy

54 Understanding the importance of key

1 yellow = epicentre of earthquake, red = Indonesia

2 key person = British schoolgirl; key action = raised the alert; two key sentences = A ten-year-old .... The beach and hotel were evacuated ...

3 tourists, volunteers to help after disaster

55 How to make a storyboard

1 eg. 1935 builds up army (hand adding another soldier to line of soldiers), 1936 builds fleet and air force (ship and plane),1936 signs treaty with Italy and Japan (3 hands labelled Germany, Italy, Japan all joined together),1936 helps Spanish rebels (soldier labelled Spanish rebel, 'V', soldier labelled Spanish Govt. + Germany above Spanish rebel), 1938 takes Austria (hand grabbing outline of Austria),1939 seizes Czechoslovakia (hand grabbing outline of Czechoslovakia),1939 signs treaty with Russia (two hands labelled Germany and Russia shaking), 1939 marches into Poland (soldiers crossing line called Poland), War (2 heads labelled Britain and France with combined speech bubble saying 'We declare war on Germany').

2 eg. outline of NZ with people leaving, newspaper headline 'Wages cut', unemployment rate, family leaving home which has For Sale notice on it, people leaving farm which has For Sale notice on it, Sign saying 'Soup Kitchen', several people fighting, newspaper headline of 'Labour wins 1935 election'

56 Understanding historical issues

2 **a** Israel, **b** top right, **c** Egypt, Syria, Jordan, Lebanon, **d** West Bank, Gaza, **e** conflict, war, **f** has been going long time

57 How to take notes

1 1948 communists vs Brit-ruled Malaya troops. Jungle camps, ambushes, derailings, raids, killed rubber plantations owners, cut rubber trees, burned factories. British hunter-killer platoons used cunning eg. punctured food cans at purchase

2 **a** British, **b** for example, **c** communists

3 1948 Malayan communists revolt

58 Understanding what a historical investigation is

1 patience, desire for truth, discernment, determination, problem-solving, ability to gather and analyse information, ability to evaluate, research, reasoning, making connections, finding evidence, presenting a case

2 **a** log, **b** evaluate, **c** define, **d** plan, **e** inquiry, investigation, **f** rank, **g** focusing questions, **h** select

59 How to define areas of inquiry for a historical Investigation

1 eg. birth, a success, an award, marriage, driver's licence, leaving home, first job, recognition from community, retirement.

2 a, b, d, f

3 historical investigation is based on research

60 How to create focusing questions for a historical Investigation

1 **a** focus, **b** focusing, **c** focus, focusing.

2 b

3 c

4 a

61 How to plan for a historical investigation

1 **a** to look ahead, **b** just for the individual student, **c** good, **d** what type of information could be found, **e** a focused manner

2 eg. date for handing it in, tasks, timeline of milestones, where information might be found, how to keep information together

3 unless you make a plan to help you reach your goal it is likely the goal is never reached and forever remains on your wish-list

62 How to gather and select historical information

1 collected, chose, wrote, made a note in log

2 23/3/16 Took photo of pocket watch made about 1907 and trench art knife made from war shrapnel that belonged to 'Uncle Harry' on my father's side of the family, when Harry was at Gallipoli in 1915. For focusing question 2 on what items soldiers had at Gallipoli. Chose trench art knife as it was made by Harry himself.

3 chose, photocopies, atlas, wrote, number, focusing question, a note in her log

63 How to organise historical information

2 under focusing questions, in order of gathering and selecting, under types of sources, in chronological order of events, under headings of usefulness, under location

64 How to rank historical information

1 name of source, brief description of source, how it relates to focusing questions, ranking, reason for ranking.

2 ranking shows why source is ranked first, second and third in relationship to others, eg. source 2 is said to be better than source 3 and not as good as source 1

65 How to evaluate a historical investigation

1 **a** evaluation allows you to assess and adapt actions so they can be as effective as possible, show you areas for improvement, help you reach goals more efficiently; skill that will be of help throughout life in any field **b** if you are not going to be honest in an evaluation there is no point in doing one and if you don't do one you lose chance to keep improving

Example

New Zealand has a Waitangi Tribunal to which Maori can take complaints that the Crown (government) has broken promises contained in the Treaty of Waitangi. People can give oral evidence at it such as eye-witness accounts of historical events and oral histories handed down the generations.

Such oral evidence may be able to show feelings and emotions better than other forms such as written or visual evidence, and also allows listeners to ask questions.

Oral evidence = evidence that is presented by word of mouth.

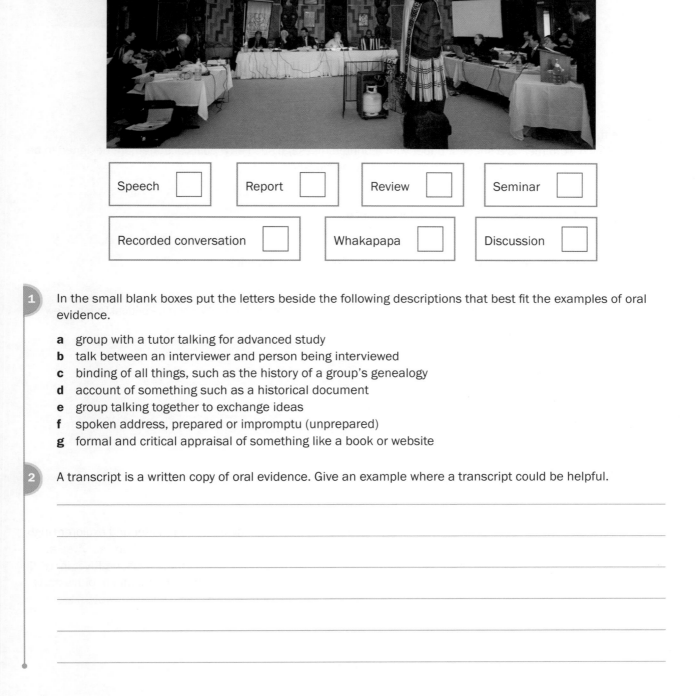

| Speech ☐ | Report ☐ | Review ☐ | Seminar ☐ |

| Recorded conversation ☐ | Whakapapa ☐ | Discussion ☐ |

1 In the small blank boxes put the letters beside the following descriptions that best fit the examples of oral evidence.

a group with a tutor talking for advanced study
b talk between an interviewer and person being interviewed
c binding of all things, such as the history of a group's genealogy
d account of something such as a historical document
e group talking together to exchange ideas
f spoken address, prepared or impromptu (unprepared)
g formal and critical appraisal of something like a book or website

2 A transcript is a written copy of oral evidence. Give an example where a transcript could be helpful.

_____

_____

_____

_____

_____

31 | How to use written historical evidence

You can use written evidence when you are studying a topic, or you can create your own written evidence when you write answers to questions.

> Written evidence = evidence presented through the medium of writing, such as documents and websites.

1   Use the images to help you answer the following.

   a   Which word means a sheet of paper with a printed message such as a political statement designed to be nailed up in a village square or distributed among citizens?

   _____

   b   Name five sources of written historical evidence.

   _____

   c   Give one difference between the 1969 newspaper and one of today?

   _____

   d   Which image is most likely to have the following caption: Created by the Women's Political Union, New York City, January 28, 1911?

   _____

   e   What does IOT stand for?

   _____

   f   What is a logbook?

   _____

   g   Why is a letter classed as written evidence?

   _____

2   In 2016 the movie *The Revenant* won many awards. It was based on the American hunter and explorer Hugh Glass. A letter that Glass wrote to the parents of another fur trapper who was killed by Indians survives and some of his superiors mention his name in their papers. A bear savaged Glass on the Missouri River in 1823 and, badly wounded, he crawled and staggered over 300 km to get vengeance on the members of his party who left him behind. Although there was no eyewitness account of the bear attack, a lawyer wrote a story about it and it appeared in newspapers and journals.

   a   Underline the sentence with two pieces of evidence that prove Glass existed.
   b   Circle or highlight five sources of written evidence.

Visual historical evidence = something that appeals to the sense of sight and is used to illustrate and help understanding of something like a historical event.

Examples

Cartoons	Photographs	Advertisements	Timelines
Films	Posters	Graphs	Drawings	Maps
Charts	Paintings	PowerPoint slides	Diagrams

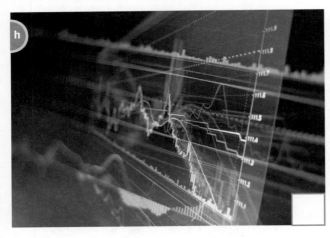

"I am here to interview.
How gentle is the corporate culture?"

1 In the blank boxes on the visuals put letters to show which of the following descriptions best fits them.

a Clash of time-zones.

b 3D with photographic projection.

c 1933 party rally in Nuremberg.

d Recruitment poster.

e About location.

f 1869 advertisement.

g 1924 child labour.

h At an archeological site.

i Useful data.

j Female warriors.

2 State what kind or kinds of visual would be best suited to show the following.

a Dates of important events between World War 1 and World War 2.

_____

b The funny side of a politician's error. _____

c Progress of tropical cyclone Winston across the Pacific. _____

d A protest march against a government mining proposal. _____

e How Ancient Romans carried water in aqueducts into distant towns.

_____

f The layout of a Maori fighting pa of the 1840s. _____

g The naval Battle of Trafalgar in 1805. _____

Analyse = to examine something carefully in order to discover its essential features and meaning.

Example

The setting is the dining table of a rich banker.

The banker is exaggeratedly big and powerful.

The banker is well-dressed with top hat, overcoat and monocle.

The wad of banknotes is a symbol of wealth.

The banker is ready to eat the world.

Red suggests drama and an important event.

The facial expression of the banker shows contentment and disregard for the worker beneath.

The graph is a symbol of a downturn that has led to economic depression.

As a result of the depression, the worker is only just hanging on by the fingernails.

The worker is disproportionately much smaller than the banker.

The upward straining face of the worker suggests desperation.

The message is that the depression has hit workers much harder than those with money and power and the latter are doing nothing to help workers.

1 State the message of this 1914 cartoon and some ways it delivered it.

_____

_____

_____

_____

_____

_____

_____

On 2 August 1914, Germany demanded that its armies be allowed to go through neutral Belgium as it wanted to get to Paris quickly. Belgium refused. Germany invaded and Britain declared war on Germany.

BRAVO, BELGIUM !

2 State the message of the cartoon and some ways it delivered it.

_____

_____

_____

_____

_____

_____

_____

_____

_____

WOMAN'S "SPHERE"

FASHION

GOSSIP

Woman Devotes Her Time to Gossip and Clothes Because She Has Nothing Else to Talk About. Give Her Broader Interests and She Will Cease to Be Vain and Frivolous.

This 1909 cartoon refers to a time when females in many countries were not allowed to vote and were expected to be interested in so-called female interests rather than politics.

3 Look at the cartoon and answer the questions.

a What is the name of the cartoonist?

_____

_____

b Why has he divided his cartoon into two?

_____

_____

1939

Germany Czechoslovakia

Brockie

2014

Russia

Ukraine

c Which two countries are being active?

_____

d Which two countries are being passive (non-active)?

_____

e How are the two active countries portrayed?

_____

f Are their actions best described as friendly or unfriendly?

_____

g Give a reason for your answer to the last question.

_____

h What does the cartoonist suggest will happen next?

 ISBN: 9780170389334

Performance = delivering historical evidence in front of an audience through forms such as mime, play, waiata, role play, practical demonstration, and staging a tableau – a group of motionless people showing a historical scene.

If you were commemorating Anzac Day you might see some of these performances.

- A play from a dramatic society about how the Anzac legend began.
- A brass-band concert of Anzac-themed music.
- The story of the Maori Battalion from a school kapa haka group.
- Museum volunteers acting aloud the words of New Zealanders who fought at Gallipoli.
- Actors performing poems by famous war poets such as Wilfred Owen.
- A symphony orchestra and choir programme about the Gallipoli landings.
- A workshop demonstration of how to make poppies from tissue paper.
- A First World War dance by a performing arts group.
- A contingent of riders and their horses enacting the Gallipoli landing.
- A sound and light show featuring noises of guns and orders to soldiers.
- A special dawn service including songs, conch music and the *Last Post*.
- A demonstration of how to make models of Gallipoli trench systems.
- A musical revue about soldiers at the front.
- A parade featuring military personnel and vintage war machinery.

1 Highlight or underline all the different forms of performance historical evidence mentioned in this unit.

2 State what form of performance evidence you could best use to show the following.

a How early Pakeha settlers made clothes from sacks.

_____

b An argument between a male and female about females getting the vote that ends with a chase involving an umbrella.

_____

c A group of Maori chiefs discussing whether or not to sign the Treaty of Waitangi.

_____

d A moment in the life of a school student in 1900.

_____

How to use appropriate format and style

Format = how information is set out. Features include shape, size, typeface, font. The format of newspapers 100 years ago was different to that of modern newspapers.

Style = how something is written, spoken or performed, depending on things such as time, place and audience. Formal style uses some or all of the following: no slang, proper grammar, not personal, no abbreviations or contractions such as 'NZ' and 'wasn't', longer sentences, third person point of view (he, she, they). Informal style uses some or all of the following: more like spoken conversation, more personal, abbreviations and contractions, shorter sentences, first person point of view (I, we).

Appropriate = suitable, fitting, such as using the right behaviour or language for a particular location and time. The opposite of appropriate is inappropriate.

1 In the blank boxes below the images, put a number of 1 to 4 to show which is likely to involve the most formal style (1) going down to the most informal style (4).

☐ ☐ ☐ ☐

2 Fill in the gaps in the following.

If you were asked to create a newspaper story about the Tangiwai disaster of 1953 that killed 151 people when a bridge collapsed and a train plunged into the Whangaehu River, you would have to think about _____ format and _____. The _____ would be a short, attention-grabbing but dignified few _____ about the event, the lead _____ would include the who, _____, where, why, when and how, and any extra paragraphs would contain further _____ such as eye-witness _____. Because the event was a _____, the tone of the story would be _____, and because it was in the pre-_____ age, nobody would have been scrambling for _____ to ring loved ones.

3 Put F (for formal) or I (for informal) after each of the following to show what style they are most likely to be.

a Student discussion about local history _____

b Text message _____

c 1840 Treaty of Waitangi _____

d Act of Parliament _____

e Principal's address at prize-giving _____

f Legal document _____

g Diary of a prisoner of war _____

h Minutes of a meeting _____

i History book for university students _____

j Email _____

k Birth certificate _____

l Comic strip _____

   ISBN: 9780170389334

Step 1 = Observation. Note the different features such as colour or shading and texture, people, symbols, words, setting, time, place, action, facial expressions, dress, details given in photograph's caption.

Step 2 = Inference. Think about what you can conclude from your observations such as why the photograph was taken or why the poster was created, what it suggests about the era.

Example

Observation = Teenage girl cooking on stove that is basic but better technology than open fire. Kitchen utensils hanging from nails on walls. Bare floorboards, bare walls. Girl's clothes torn and threadbare.

Inference = Girl standing in for mother (mother was actually in a tuberculosis sanitarium). Suggestive of poverty and a 1930s scene (it was taken during the Great Depression of the 1930s and the father was a poor farmer).

1

a State four features you observe.

_____

_____

_____

b State two things you infer.

_____

_____

_____

2

a State four features you observe.

_____

_____

_____

_____

b State two things you infer. (Clue = building is 102-storey skyscraper opened in 1931.)

_____

_____

How to recognise setting

Setting = the location and time in which an event takes place.

Examples

Setting = World War 1, known at the time as the Great War, took place from 1914 to 1918. Most, of the action was in Europe, such as the dogfight between these pilots in a British two-seater monoplane and a German Taube fighter.

Setting = This is the ruins of the Philippeion temple in Ancient Olympia. It was a setting for the original Olympic Games. Warfare was a constant feature of the Ancient Greek lifestyle. Peace broke out every four years during the month when the Olympic Games took place. The Greek states agreed that they would stop fighting to let people travel to and from Olympia for the Games.

1 In the following events, chosen at random from the beginning of 2016, underline or highlight information that helps you recognise the settings.

a Jan 4 Colombo's Gemology Institute certifies the world's largest ever blue star sapphire, found in a Sri Lankan mine.

b Jan 5 15-year-old Mumbai schoolboy becomes the first batsman to score 1000 runs in a single cricket innings when he made 1009 not out at an inter-school match at Kalyan.

c Jan 6 The North Korean Government stated it had successfully tested a thermonuclear weapon.

d Jan 6 *Star Wars: The Force Awakens*, breaks US box office record.

e Jan 16 First ever flower grown in space aboard the International Space Station.

f Feb 4 King of Morocco switches on world's largest solar plant near Ouarzazate.

g Feb 23 Awaroa Inlet beach in the Abel Tasman put in hands of all New Zealanders after crowdfunding buys it.

h Feb 29 Mega pop star Adele begins her world tour in Belfast, Northern Ireland.

2 This event is a tornado in Oklahoma, USA. Describe the setting.

_____

_____

_____

_____

_____

_____

Historical context = the circumstances such as attitudes, beliefs, behaviour and conditions that existed at a certain time and which help people today understand the past event better.

If you were asked to write a diary entry for someone in Europe who witnessed a Black Death plague of the 14th century, you would need to think of the historical context. At that time there was no modern technology such as computers, and nobody knew what caused the plague. You might imagine you were a plague doctor who wore a mask with glass eyes and a beak filled with straw and scented plant material to protect yourself from bad air, which you mistakenly believed was a cause.

1 Put the following 15 boxes into sets of three. Each set has an image, an event, and a context. Show the sets by numbers in the blank boxes.

In 2002, SARS (Severe Acute Respiratory Syndrome) broke out in China. By early 2003 it was spreading around the world with many deaths reported. People could not understand how China knew about SARS for months before it let the world know.

Many ancient cultures believed the Earth was flat.

In 1955, a black woman called Rosa Parks on a bus in Montgomery, Alabama, refused to give up her seat to a white person when the driver asked her to do so. This event sparked the US civil rights movement.

Many people in medieval Europe believed females who practised herbal medicine were witches and deserved to be burned at the stake.

Lack of knowledge and technology had people using expressions such as 'the four corners of the world' and 'the sun sank into the sea.'

In 1914 many young men saw the Great War as a grand adventure.

Human rights and tolerance were centuries away; anyone with special powers was often considered wicked. □	The pace of life was much slower and war was a way to see the world. Many believed it was glorious to die for your country. □	Racial segregation and discrimination, especially against African Americans, and especially in the South, was the norm for society. □

The country's culture of silence, the shortage of hospitals and doctors, and its vast population, many of whom lived in poor rural areas, contributed to a slow reaction.

□

2 Read the following, think about the context, and answer the question.

On July 17, 1918, while Russia was in the midst of revolution and society was in an uproar, revolutionaries hurriedly murdered the Romanov Tsar Nicholas II, his wife and their five children, and buried them in secret. Afterwards, many people believed rumours that the youngest daughter, Anastasia, had survived and imposters claiming to be Anastasia were actually her. How could they have believed that?

_____

_____

_____

_____

_____

3 Read the following, think about the context, and answer the question.

In 2016 in New Zealand the TV show *The Bachelor* featured girls in bikinis and strapless dresses and ended up with the bachelor presenting the final rose to his choice of the girl of his dreams, and then dumping her the next day when he visited her in her hotel.

In 1816 in England's genteel society, females appeared in public in floor-length skirts, long sleeves and high collars and often had their husbands chosen for them by parents. If a man presented a rose to a girl it would have to have been in the company of the girl's chaperone. A girl would not stay in a hotel and receive a male visitor by herself. Departures from these rules would cause a huge scandal.

How does this help explain why females in 1816 England were not allowed to vote but females in 2016 New Zealand were?

_____

_____

_____

_____

Perspective = the way you see something, what makes you see and understand things like events, sources, issues and ideas in the particular way that you do. For example, if you had lost a friend in a tsunami, your perspective on the news that your class is going to study the history of natural disasters might be different to that of another person.

Examples of factors that can influence perspective

Culture (Pakeha, Maori, Chinese)
Status or mana (respected, hated, tolerated)
Socio-economic position (rich, poor, average)
Groups (Ku Klux Klan, Hitler Youth, online games)
Life experiences (climate change, migration, war)
Religion (Muslim, Christian, no religion)

Gender (female, male, transgender)
Age (13, 23, 33)
Country (NZ, China, Peru)
Education (none, little, much)
Work (IT, student, labourer)
Time (1816, 1916, 2016)

1 Give one or more factors that might cause two different perspectives in the following.

a An illiterate peasant and a studious monk at the time of the invention of the printing press about 1440.

_____

b A Jewish scholar's history of Jerusalem and a Muslim scholar's history of Jerusalem.

_____

c Eye-witness accounts of May 6, 1937 *Hindenburg* passenger airship disaster from a surviving passenger and a short-sighted observer.

_____

d Quotes from a 16-year-old and his grandmother about a rap song on the history of rap.

_____

e Accounts in history books of 1860 and 2016 about Ngapuhi chief Hone Heke chopping down the flagpole in the mid-1840s.

_____

f Letters home from a New Zealand soldier and a Turkish soldier at Gallipoli in 1915.

_____

2 Make a note in the blank boxes about what each suggests about perspective.

"Our Innovation Department is looking for someone with a child-like perspective."

How to get into role

Getting into role = imagining yourself as someone else at a particular time and changing the way you behave, dress, speak or write in order to show you understand the life and times of that person.

Example

In 1915, during World War One, a German submarine off the coast of Ireland torpedoed the British ship *Lusitania*. Over a thousand people drowned.

A survivor pleaded for the US to join the war effort against Germany, saying 'Remember the *Lusitania*.'

The editor of a British newspaper was furious at the attack on 'innocent and defenceless people'.

Kapitänleutnant Schweiger of the German submarine was pleased at his success.

The US President sent four protests to the German Kaiser.

A steward said the passengers were at lunch when the attack came, officials acted bravely, and the sinking ship was a dreadful sight.

American millionaire Alfred Vanderbilt, who drowned, gave his life-jacket to a young woman even though he could not swim.

The editor of a German newspaper claimed the ship had been armed with guns and was carrying war materials.

Kaiser Wilhelm II later pledged an end to Germany's unrestricted submarine warfare against unarmed passenger ships.

1 State which character you would choose to role-play if you wanted to be the following.

a   An American hero. _____

b   A person justifying the attack. _____

c   A ship employee. _____

d   A naval commander. _____

e   An emperor. _____

f   Someone trying to stop US being neutral.

g   Someone condemning the attack. _____

h   The leader of a neutral country. _____

2 State what else this person might need to do in order to get totally into role.

_____

_____

_____

_____

This person is dressed as a member of the Knight Templars, the best fighters from European countries such as England, Scotland and France from the 12th to the 14th century.

   ISBN: 9780170389334

A movement = PEOPLE in a group ACTING to get CHANGE.

Example

Scenes in Dien Bien Phu in Vietnam are peaceful
today but in 1953 thousands were killed in a battle there between French troops, who ruled Vietnam at that time,
and a movement called Viet Minh made up of Vietnamese (PEOPLE) fighting (ACTING) to free Vietnam from French
rule (CHANGE).

Dien Bien Phu
Today

Dien Bien Phu
1953

Examples of movements

Anti-apartheid	Anti-slavery	Civil rights	Environmental
Hippie	Hitler Youth	Kingitanga	Kotahitanga
Occupy Wall Street	Mau	Muslim League	Peace
Pro-life	Satyagraha	Slow Food	Sons of Liberty
Suffrage	Taleban	Temperance	Young Italy

Aims of Movements

Abortions stopped. _____

Abolition of slavery. _____

The right to vote for women. _____

Social and economic equality. _____

Equality for African Americans. _____

Italian states joined as one. _____

Election of Maori King to unite tribes. _____

Young people to become loyal Nazis. _____

Rights for Muslims in largely Hindu India. _____

Stopping sale and consumption of alcohol. _____

Getting rid of British rule of American colonies. _____

Conservation, sustainable use of resources. _____

Eradication of weapons of mass destruction. _____

Sustainable food, promoting local businesses. _____

Abolition of separation of races in South Africa. _____

Parliamentary Maori unity on non-tribal grounds. _____

Islamic fundamentalists in Afghanistan waging war. _____

Harmony with nature, communal living, music, drugs. _____

Non-violent opposition to get rid of British rule in India. _____

Independence from New Zealand for Western Samoa. _____

1 Beside the 'Aims of movements' put the names from the 'Examples of movements' box that best fit.

2 Name features that movements have in common. Use the graphic below to help you say how others might react to a movement.

_____

_____

_____

_____

_____

_____

_____

_____

_____

_____

Understanding a social force

A social force = a feature in society that can change ideas and influence people.

Social networking is a social force. People using internet-based social media programmes to make connections and communications with other people can change ideas and influence people.

1 Put the best-fit names from the box beside the following descriptions of social forces.

a whole community sharing work and property _____

b looking after the environment and resources _____

c demanding independence for and devotion to a country _____

d government of country by its own people _____

e treating different races differently _____

f creating an empire by taking over other lands _____

g changing from agrarian to manufacturing _____

h all about mechanic or virtual artificial agents _____

i wanting equal rights for females _____

j use or threat of unlawful violence to cause fear _____

k seeing the universe as having a special purpose _____

l different cultures coexisting with equal rights _____

m political or religious views furthest from the centre _____

n shift of population from countryside to town _____

o big businesses developing international influence _____

industrialisation	globalisation	racism	religion	terrorism
communism	urbanisation	feminism	democracy	extremism
nationalism	sustainability	imperialism	multiculturalism	robotics

2 In the blank boxes, put the name of a social force that best fits the images.

ISBN: 9780170389334   PHOTOCOPYING OF THIS PAGE IS RESTRICTED UNDER LAW.

59

Understanding action

Action = something done or being done, usually to achieve an aim.

This poster shows a famous action of World War Two – the raising of the US flag during the Battle of Iwo Jima on 23 February 1945. About 23,000 Japanese defended the island from a network of tunnels, caves and underground facilities but after a month of fighting, the US marines captured the island.

1 For each image give one action for which the person is famous.

Robin Hood

Mother Theresa

Sir Edmund Hillary

William Shakespeare

_____

_____

_____

Wright Brothers

Helen Keller

Florence Nightingale

Joan of Arc

_____

_____

_____

2 Underline all the actions in the following.

Isis, Islamic State of Iraq and the Levant, or just Islamic State, said an aim was to establish a global caliphate by bringing all the Muslim inhabited areas of the world under its rule. It took control of territory in Syria and Iraq, and in other places such as Afghanistan and Libya. It trained its fighters in guerrilla warfare and to use social networks and the internet to spread propaganda, to recruit fighters from around the world and to show videos of beheadings it carried out. It took military equipment from many places such as weapons stockpiles in Iraq, ruined some historical sites in the Middle East, and displaced millions of people from their homes and turned them into refugees and migrants. It ignored the Declaration of Human Rights by actions such as using child soldiers. It caused other countries to wage war against it.

Historical conventions = ways of doing, saying, writing and seeing things that were common at the time.

Examples

New Zealand used to be a British colony, so the convention of measurement was the British imperial system. A 1976 Act of Parliament finished the changing over to the metric system. From then on, for example, people had to remember that the convention of a 25-yard line was now the 22-metres line, 50 miles was now 80 kilometres and fruit was now measured by kilograms instead of pounds and ounces.

Likewise, New Zealand used to have the convention of imperial currency until it adopted decimal currency in 1967. From then on, people had to remember that the convention of counting money in pounds, shillings and pence was wrong and they had to count in dollars and cents.

Until recently the most usual convention for showing dates of years before the year 0 was BC (Before Christ) and for dates of years after the year 0 it was AD (Anno Domini, In the year of the Lord). Now a different convention, thought to be more culturally neutral for non-Christians, is becoming popular - BCE (Before the Common Era) instead of BC, and CE (Common Era) instead of AD. Neither version includes a year zero. BC/AD is the same as BCE/CE so 2016 CE matches AD 2016 and 300 BCE matches 300 BC.

Early Europeans had the convention of referring to the indigenous people of New Zealand as natives. In 1947 official use of the term 'natives' stopped and was replaced by 'Maori'. For example, the Department of Native Affairs became the Department of Maori Affairs.

Early Europeans tended to use the English convention of adding an 's' to Maori to show the plural. Official documents today usually use Maori as the plural, following the Maori language convention which did not use 's'.

One pound = £1 = 20 shillings = 240 pennies = 2 dollars.

One shilling = 1/- = 12 pennies or pence = 10 cents.

Sixpence = 6d = 6 pennies or pence = 5 cents.

Ten shillings = 120 pennies = 1 dollar.

1 Answer the questions.

a For what might the five items in the first image on page 61 have been used?

_____

b At what speed in miles per hour is the car going?

_____

c How many cents would have made five shillings?

_____

d In what year did the money in the image become legal?

_____

e How many pennies would have made 20 cents?

_____

f What is another convention for AD?

_____

g What convention for measuring French fries would have been used in 1950?

_____

h An article about a haka performed by the natives would most likely have appeared in 1867 or 1997?

_____

i How many dollars would have made £5?

_____

j What does BCE with dates stand for?

_____

2 Name conventions, such as dress and behaviour, shown in this Victorian image.

_____

_____

_____

Relevant = to do with the subject. The opposite is irrelevant.

In the following, all sentences except one are about the subject, the sinking of the *Titanic*. The underlined sentence is off-subject. It is not relevant.

The Sinking of the *Titanic*

The *Titanic* was the largest and most luxurious liner of its day and its owners claimed it was unsinkable. In 1912 it set sail from England bound for New York and in the Atlantic Ocean it hit an iceberg. <u>Leonardo diCaprio, who starred in a movie about the *Titanic*, is a Hollywood star and he won an Oscar in 2016 for a role in another movie.</u> The *Titanic* sank swiftly. There were not enough lifeboats for everyone and more than 1500 people died.

1 Make relevant comments about this 1942 poster. ——→

_____

_____

2 Underline the sentence in each of the following that is not relevant.

Hunters searched for a leopard that escaped from Auckland Zoo one day in 1925. Many parents kept their children home from school and the City Council offered a reward for the return of the animal, dead or alive. The cheetah is sometimes called the hunting leopard. There were false alarms. Policemen argued about the best way to get the leopard down from a tree until they realised the animal they had cornered was a possum.

A 27-year-old in 1962 became the first person to have a recorded swim of Cook Strait. He swam from Cape Terawhiti in the North Island to Wellington Rock in the South Island. He had to battle for almost 11 and a quarter hours against cold and vicious rips. Someone gave him a spanner when he reached land. He chipped off a piece of rock to prove his crossing. Swimming is good for asthmatics because it helps breathing techniques.

One day in 1880 a train climbed Siberia Hill on the Wellington Rimutaka line. This was 40 years after the Treaty of Waitangi when there were no trains. Suddenly, a gust of wind caught the train. It blew carriages and a van off the tracks and hurled them over a cliff. Three people were killed and 20 injured. Doctors were brought in on a special train. They had to crawl to reach survivors.

One day in 1907 fire broke out in Wellington's wooden Parliament. Firemen fought the blaze for four hours. Many books, documents and historic paintings went up in flames. The bell rang all the time because the wires had fused. Years later the Reichstag fire burned the German Parliament and people blamed the Nazis.

How to recognise bias

Bias = having prejudice; having a strong one-sided feeling for or against, usually an unreasonable or unfair feeling. If you let your personal feelings overtake critical thinking, you are being biased.

Example

Julius Caesar was biased towards Cleopatra because he admired beauty and she was considered beautiful.

Mark Antony's wife was biased against Cleopatra because Mark Antony had a romantic relationship with Cleopatra.

History sources can be biased by telling only what the creator thought happened or wants other people to think happened. A reader needs to be on high alert and asking questions such as the following.

Who created the source and why? Did the creator want to inform people or to persuade people? Did the creator have a hidden agenda? Did the creator use emotive words designed to make people think a certain way?

Did the creator mention different viewpoints or is it all a one-sided viewpoint?

Put a cross beside the sentences about Robert the Bruce that seem to be biased.

a   Hiding in a cave from his English hunters was typical Scottish idiocy.

b   Legend says he was inspired to keep fighting the English by watching a spider spin its web.

c   He was crowned King of Scotland in 1306.

d   His victory at the Battle of Bannockburn in 1314 was due to nothing but luck.

e   Leprosy is an awful fate so let us hope it is true that he died of leprosy.

Answer the questions about the image of the mother holding the son's school report.

a   Give reasons why the report aims to be an unbiased document.

_____

_____

_____

_____

b   Write one comment from either the mother or the son that shows bias.

_____

Ambiguity = having two or more possible meanings, which creates doubt or uncertainty in a listener, reader or viewer.

Examples

- The French teacher took an instant liking to his bright pupil Archimedes. (Was the teacher from France or did the teacher teach French as a subject? Or both?)
- Queen Mary had her bottom scraped. (There was a queen called Queen Mary and a ship called *Queen Mary*.)

Historic headlines

Man eating piranha mistakenly sold as pet fish.
Arson suspect is held in fire.
Officials put foot down on dog waste.
Local high school dropouts cut in half.
Genetic engineering splits scientists.
Squad helps dog bite victim.
Grandmother of eight makes hole in one.
Lawmen from Mexico barbecue guests.

1 Say why you should always try to avoid being ambiguous in your written work.

_____

_____

2 Use as few changes as possible to make the following no longer ambiguous.

a In an effort to kill a bee Ben Hur drove his chariot into a tree.

_____

b Friar Tuck had been riding for three months when he fell asleep and crashed his horse.

_____

c After the President watched the chimp perform, he was taken to Queen Street and fed two buckets full of bananas.

_____

d Sue Smith visited the school and lectured on 'Nasty Pests'. A lot were present.

_____

e The Governor-General smashed the champagne against the prow and the crowd cheered as she slid down the runway into the tide.

_____

f Protestors released rats in Parliament and these were arrested when they left.

_____

g Porn took centre stage at the Supreme Court.

_____

How to distinguish between fact and opinion

You might expect that what this female says next is going to be a fact, a piece of information that can be proved true, such as 'The Treaty of Waitangi was signed in 1840.' However, she might instead give an opinion, a comment that expresses her own feeling or belief and which cannot be proved true or false, such as 'The Treaty of Waitangi is an interesting topic and we should all study it.' Her fact contains data – the date – and statements that contain data tend to be facts, as long as the facts have the details correct. Her opinion contains beliefs; not everyone believes the Treaty is interesting and that we should all study it. Comments that use descriptive words to appeal to your emotions and try to convince you of something tend to be opinions.

Example

Jonno says, 'New Zealand sent an engineering unit and a medical team to the Vietnam War in 1964 and an artillery battalion in 1965.' THAT IS A FACT because Jonno can prove it is true by showing it filed in official records, talking to people who went to Vietnam as part of the teams, and by showing it pictured in newsreels of the time.

Lara says, 'New Zealand should not have got involved in the Vietnam War.' THAT IS AN OPINION because Lara cannot prove it is true as many people do not agree with her and she is saying what she thinks should not have happened, rather than what did happen.

1 Cross out some words that Lara said so you can change her opinion into a fact.

2 Write F (for fact) or O (for opinion) in the following comments about Michael Joseph Savage, who was a famous New Zealand Prime Minister.

> He was short and strong. ☐

> He is the best leader the country has had. ☐

> He immigrated to New Zealand in 1907. ☐

> His public speeches were the greatest made in New Zealand. ☐

> He became Prime Minister when Labour won the 1935 election. ☐

> He was born in Australia. ☐

> His mother died when he was five. ☐

> For a while he cut flax in the Manawatu swamp. ☐

> He signed his own death warrant when he put off a cancer operation until after the 1938 election. ☐

> He was wrong to publicly criticise Britain for accepting Hitler's taking over part of Czechoslovakia. ☐

How to avoid anachronisms

Anachronism = representation of something or someone in the wrong time. It could be anything, such as an object, something said, music, a technology, an idea.

Smartphones had not been invented at the time this person, dressed up as a Caribbean pirate, is trying to show. The anachronism has ruined his role-play.

Another example is an artist painting a village feast in 1600 England in which children eat ice cream in cones. That is an anachronism because, although a form of ice cream had been invented possibly as early as 500 BC in Asia, it is unlikely to have been in English villages and certainly not in cones because they were not invented until the late 19th century.

1 Say what anachronisms you can find in the cartoon.

_____

_____

_____

_____

_____

_____

_____

_____

2 Say what people would mean today when they accuse someone of being an anachronistic Luddite.

_____

_____

_____

_____

_____

_____

_____

_____

_____

This 1812 engraving shows Luddites breaking machines in a textile factory. Luddites were English workers who, fearing they would lose jobs, protested against the new technologies.

ISBN: 9780170389334   PHOTOCOPYING OF THIS PAGE IS RESTRICTED UNDER LAW.

Understanding chronology

Chronology = a record of events in the order in which they happened.

Example

The capture of Australian outlaw Ned Kelly in 1880 had so many twists and turns that if the story was not told in chronological order it would be difficult to understand.

Ned decided to ambush the train that was carrying the policemen who were after him. He and his gang forced railwaymen to tear up the track just out of the station at Glenrowan. The gang rounded up people from town as hostages and held them at the hotel where they all began to party. The local schoolteacher escaped and flagged the train down to warn the police. Early in the morning the police began to battle with the gang. Ned put on his metal armour and slipped out of the back of the hotel. At dawn, he loomed up behind the police line. Policemen fired but the bullets bounced off Ned's armour. Finally, a bullet hit Ned's unarmoured leg.

_____

_____

_____

1 Write what would be a good last sentence for the chronological order of the capture of Ned Kelly.

2 The following are milestones in the life of French heroine Joan of Arc who came to the rescue when France was fighting a war called The 100 Year War against England. Put the milestones into chronological order in the boxes.

A As Joan had never seen the Dauphin, he stood among his nobles to test her.

B After Orleans, Joan led France to many victories.

C In 1429 she returned and persuaded the Commandant to give her permission to go to the Dauphin.

D The English put Joan on trial. Called a witch, she was accused of wearing male clothing, and disobeying her parents and the teaching of the church.

E When she was 16, Joan went to the Commandant of a town near her village and asked him to send her to the Dauphin. He sent her home.

F She was born in France in 1412.

G Joan picked the Dauphin out immediately among the nobles and she was given command of an army to go and help Orleans, which the English were attacking. She put on armour, inspired the troops to follow her and saved Orleans.

H In 1430, French soldiers, fighting on the side of the English, captured Joan and sold her to the English.

I Joan was burned at the stake in 1431.

J At 12 years old, Joan began to hear voices and see visions of saints who told her she must go to the French court and help the Dauphin, the heir to the throne.

 ISBN: 9780170389334

Obituary = a notice of the death of a person. Longer obituaries include details of the person's life. You may be asked to write an obituary of a person, real or fictional.

Points to think about when writing an obituary.

Full name of person.	Nickname/s.	Date of birth.	Place of birth.	Date of death.	Place of death.	Job title.

Richard Seddon 1845 – 1906

Richard John Seddon is dead. He died suddenly in office on board ship on 10 June 1906. He was on his way back to New Zealand after a visit to Sydney. He is survived by his wife, daughters and sons.

Born in England in 1845, he became our Premier in 1893. So popular was he, we called him King Dick; he in turn called us 'God's Own Country'. As he told a Maori gathering once, like Mount Egmont and Mount Ruapehu he was a fixture in the New Zealand landscape.

Although both parents were teachers, young Richard was seen to be a poor student and he left school at the age of twelve. Rumours later went round Parliament that he could not read until he was thirty. He had once been a miner and pub-keeper on the West Coast and he was often accused of providing 'jobs for the boys'; one story tells of how he made a government department hire a West Coaster and when the head of the department sent a memo complaining that the man could neither read nor write, Seddon wrote in its margin, 'Then learn him.'

A large man, Seddon was just under six feet tall. His nickname of 'Old Leather Lungs' referred to the bellow with which he made his many long speeches. He told an audience once that he had been called a fraud. If he was, he said, he was a big one because last week he turned the scales at nineteen stone and six pounds.

Seddon was against Asian immigration into New Zealand. He stopped the Chinese here from getting the Old-Age Pension he had introduced in 1898. He called gum-diggers from Dalmatia 'a plague of locusts'.

When some thought the best way to stop youths under seventeen smoking in public places was not a whipping and a fine but for grown men to stop, Seddon gave up his cigars ...

Family still alive.	Early life.	Stature.	Belief/s.	Quote/s.	Formal language.	Conventions of the time.

1   Draw arrows from the side boxes to an example of each one in the obituary.

2   If Seddon died yesterday, give three examples of conventions in his obituary that would be different to those of 1906.

_____

_____

How to use a timeline

Timeline = events set out in a pattern, in chronological or reverse-chronological order, and often in the present tense (I *win* Lotto).

Evel Knievel

1939	Born Robert Knievel in Montana.
1965	Forms Evel Knievel's Motorcycle Daredevils.
1966	Begins touring alone.
1968	Crashes while jumping fountains at Caesar's Palace in Las Vegas.
1970	Clears 13 cars in a jump.
1971	Clears 19 cars in a jump.
1973	Clears 50 cars in a jump.
1975	Clears 13 double-decker buses in London.
1976	Injured while jumping tank of live sharks in Chicago.
2007	Dies.

Communism

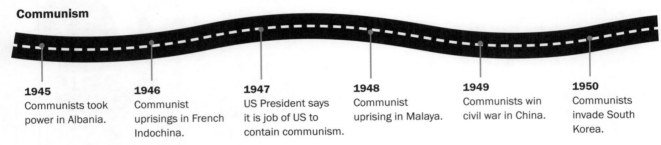

1945
Communists took power in Albania.

1946
Communist uprisings in French Indochina.

1947
US President says it is job of US to contain communism.

1948
Communist uprising in Malaya.

1949
Communists win civil war in China.

1950
Communists invade South Korea.

Modern Summer Olympics

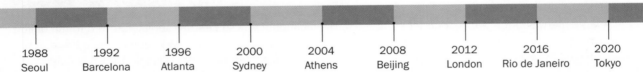

1988	1992	1996	2000	2004	2008	2012	2016	2020
Seoul	Barcelona	Atlanta	Sydney	Athens	Beijing	London	Rio de Janeiro	Tokyo

1 Make some generalisations about timelines you can see from the three examples.

_____

_____

_____

2 Put the following on to a timeline.

NZ company Rex debuted pair of bionic legs in 2010; IBM computer beat world chess champion in 1997; 2013 Kirobo, world's first talking humanoid astronaut, said its first words; Honda debuted ASIMO in 2000; Roomba robotic vacuum cleaner of 2002 launched; First *Star Wars* movie in 1977 with human future shared with robots; First self-replicating robot produced in 2005.

Historians put labels on particular times to make it easier to identify them. General terms include **antiquity** (any ancient time), **decade** (10 years), **score** (20 years), **era** (period of time such as the disco era), and **period** (a block of time such as the Early Modern Period, which includes things like the Golden Age of Piracy). Sometimes terms are used interchangeably; for example, some geographical periods are called eras, epochs, ages and eons.

Prehistory	before written history
Ancient history	up to fall of Roman Empire in AD 476
Medieval history **Middle Ages**	up to about 15th century
Modern history	up to present

Stone Age	tools and weapons of stone
Copper Age	some tools and weapons of copper
Bronze Age	bronze (copper + tin) weapons and tools
Iron Age	production and use of iron

The Renaissance in Europe was a revival of culture and learning from Middle Ages to 17th century.

Age is another way of labelling a distinct period of history.

The Ice Age/s: extreme cooling of Earth's climate where ice sheets expanded.

The Dark Ages: Early Middle Ages from about 5th to 10th centuries; modern historians avoid the term as it sounds negative.

The Age of Discovery: 15th to 18th centuries when Europeans explored and discovered land.

The Elizabethan Age: reign of Queen Elizabeth I (1558–1603) in England.

The Victorian Age: reign of Queen Victoria (1837–1901) in England.

The Atomic Age: began in 1945 with atomic bombs on Hiroshima and Nagasaki.

The Space Age: began in 1957 when the Soviet Union launched Sputnik 1.

The Information Age: digital technology such as home computers in the 1970s.

1 Give words or terms from this unit that mean the following.

a A time of rebirth. _____

b A Japanese city. _____

c Event of 476 AD. _____

d One hundred years. _____

e Also called glacial ages. _____

f Before recorded history. _____

g Only the size of a beach ball. _____

h Time of European exploration. _____

i Name for reign of English Queen. _____

j Out of favour with modern historians. _____

k 1799–1815 era when Napoleon had power. _____

l Time of infamous buccaneers like Blackbeard. _____

Understanding the importance of key

Key = of great importance. For example, if you find the key idea or people in a story, it will unlock the meaning of all the other details in the story for you to understand better.

Key time　Key event　Key word　Key place　Key moment　Key idea　Key people

On Boxing Day 2004, an earthquake of magnitude 9.0, the world's biggest in 40 years, struck about 160 km off the west coast of Indonesia. It was caused when the India plate – one of the tectonic plates that make up Earth's surface – was forced under the Burma plate. The earthquake set off tsunamis that hit 12 countries in Asia such as Thailand where the famous Phuket Island was filled with thousands of overseas tourists. Amateur videos captured the 10 metre wall of water smashing into land. This extreme natural event brought months of disaster. Over 150,000 people were killed. Others were left homeless, starving, injured, sick and sad. People said it was the worst time since World War Two. Governments and individuals around the world sent money for victim relief. Some tourists stayed on to help locals.

1 Add a key below to show what the yellow concentric lines are and what the red colour shows on the map.

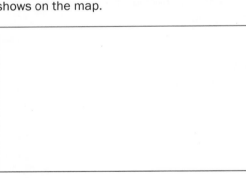

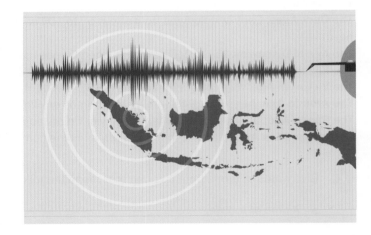

2 Underline in the following story the key person, the key action of the person, and the two key sentences that contain the result of the action.

A 10-year-old British schoolgirl saved the lives of hundreds of people after the earthquake by warning them a wall of water was about to strike. She had learned about tsunamis from her teacher at school. She was on the beach when the water went bubbly and the tide suddenly ran out. She raised the alert. The beach and hotel were evacuated before the tsunami hit.

3 Give two key ways New Zealanders could have been involved in the Boxing Day disaster.

_____

A storyboard = a rough set of drawings or outlines, often with some directions and speech, for shots planned for a film or television production. Like a comic strip, it can be a useful tool in history by using graphics to show historical events in the order they happened.

The causes of World War Two could be written like this:

In 1933 Adolph Hitler had established himself as the German leader. In 1935 he began to build up Germany's army even though a treaty signed by Germany at the end of World War One had forbidden it. In 1936 Hitler began to build a large fleet and air force, even though the treaty had also forbidden both these. In 1936 Germany got two friends by signing a treaty with Italy and Japan. In the same year, civil war broke out in Spain. Germany and Italy tried out their new weapons and planes by helping the Spanish rebels fight the government forces. In 1938 Germany took over Austria. In 1939 Germany seized Czechoslovakia and signed a treaty with Russia, and on September 1, 1939, Germany marched into Poland to take it over. Britain and France gave Hitler 24 hours to get out of Poland and when Hitler did not do so, they declared war on Germany.

Storyboard

1 Finish the storyboard for the causes of World War Two.

2 Create a storyboard for the following ideas about the Great Depression of the 1930s in New Zealand.

The number of people leaving New Zealand increased. Government cut wages of workers. Thousands of people lost their jobs. Some people lost their homes; many also lost farms. Soup kitchens opened for the hungry. There were riots in Wellington, Dunedin and Auckland. The Labour Party promised something for everyone. Labour won the 1935 election.

Storyboard

Understanding historical issues

Issues = important topics or problems in society that people think and talk about. Historical issues can be issues that are no longer in the public eye or issues that continue to cause discussion.

Examples

Bull fighting is a historical and controversial issue; the Spanish, for example, introduced the idea of a person on foot rather than the traditional person on horseback facing the bull in the early 18th century.

The death penalty, or capital punishment, which still exists in some countries, is a historical and controversial issue as it can be traced back as far as the laws of Ancient China and people still debate it today.

One way to show how people have different opinions on historical issues is by using a continuum. For example, the use of unmanned aerial vehicles (UAVs), also known as drones, continues to be a controversial issue.

Should be used | Should not be used

Two opposing extreme opinions are that military drones *should* be used as they have destroyed terrorist networks, and that military drones *should not* be used as they create more terrorists than they kill. In between those two are many more moderate opinions.

1 Mark on the continuum where your opinion is on the issue of drones used in warfare. Beside it put a reason for your answer.

2 The issue of the Israeli–Palestinian relationship has a long history of conflict between Jews and Arabs. Answer these questions.

a Name the state set up in 1948 as a Jewish nation.

_____

b Indicate which is the Palestinian flag.

c Name the four neighbouring countries drawn into the issue.

_____

d Name the two Palestinian territories (in green).

_____

e What do the silhouettes on the right side suggest?

_____

f Why is the Israel-Palestinian conflict called a historical issue?

_____

How to take notes

You can take notes about your chosen topic as you use a source such as an article or a book, or a movie or a documentary.

Reasons for taking notes
- To record information.
- To get the key points.
- To jog your memory later.
- To have a summary.

How to take notes
- Note key points only.
- Use own words where possible.
- Use abbreviations.
- Use your own shorthand.

Examples

Text

By the time World War Two ended in 1945, the United States had become the greatest power in the world. New Zealand had always believed that Britain would defend it, and especially relied on the British ships stationed at Singapore. However, the Japanese capture of Singapore from the British in 1942 made New Zealand realise it could no longer depend on Britain for protection and should instead shift its focus towards the United States.

Notes

1945 US = superpower. NZ could no longer rely on Brit after Jap took Singapore. Looked to US.

1. Underline the key points in the following and put notes from it in the box.

> In 1948 communists in Malaya tried to take over the country, which was ruled by Britain. The communists had camps in the jungle. They ambushed road traffic and derailed trains, made hit-and-run raids, killed owners of rubber plantations, cut rubber trees and burned factories. British hunter-killer platoons fought the communists in the jungle. They used cunning. An example was when anybody bought a can of food, it was then punctured so the food could not be stored and given to the communists.

2. State what these would mean in the notes taken from the text in **1** about Malaya.

a Brit _____ b e.g. _____ c coms _____

3. Summarise the first sentence in **1** in five words or fewer.

_____

_____

 ISBN: 9780170389334

> Historical investigation = a careful and thoughtful examination of a topic, such as the history of surfing, the assassination of US President Kennedy, the causes and results of the rise of Isis in Syria and Iraq, or the mysteries of the Bermuda Triangle. It is also called a historical inquiry.

Steps to follow for a historical investigation:

1 Define areas of inquiry by stating what the investigation is about.
2 Write some focusing questions to help you collect information.
3 Make a plan for how you will carry out the investigation.
4 Gather and select information from sources.
5 Keep a log to show what you have done and found.
6 Organise and rank information in order of how useful it is.
7 Use appropriate format and style to prepare your material.
8 Evaluate by saying how well it went.

1 When you are carrying out a historical investigation you are like a detective – a person after the truth of what happened. List skills that detectives and historians would have in common.

_____

_____

2 Find the words in the unit that best match the following descriptions.

a Record of actions such as that kept by a ship's captain. _____

b Judge something like a process. _____

c Show the boundaries or limits of. _____

d Step-by-step guide. _____

e Research. _____

f Put in order of importance. _____

g Designed to gather information on something specific. _____

h Carefully choose. _____

How to define areas of inquiry for a historical investigation

Defining = sorting out boundaries.
Area = set measurements or ranges.
Inquiry = research to find information on a particular topic.

Defining areas of inquiry sorts out boundaries for your investigation. For example, if you were told the historical investigation was to be a person from your local community, areas of inquiry you could define would be:

- reasons the person was living there
- milestones in the person's life
- what made the person special
- how people regarded the person at the time
- how people regard the person today
- how the person changed or helped the community.

1 Name some possible milestones of a person's life you could research.

_____

_____

_____

2 The historical investigation is the creation of Israel in 1948. Tick the best four areas of inquiry.

a Who made it a separate country. ☐   **b** Why it was created. ☐

c What caused the Six Day War of 1967. ☐   **d** What sort of country it was. ☐

e Why the Nazis killed Jews. ☐   **e** Why Israel fought a war in 1956. ☐

f The results of the creation. ☐   **f** Modern Israel today. ☐

3 The word 'enquiry' is often used interchangeably with 'inquiry' although today 'inquiry' is increasingly used to mean research. Explain why 'inquiry' is the best spelling for this unit.

_____

_____

_____

_____

Focusing (also spelt as focussing) questions = questions you make up to help you find information that will fit all the pieces of your investigation together. The questions need to be open-ended, which will let you gather a lot of information, rather than close-ended, which will just give you a very short answer.

Example

Open-ended: Why did the South African government set up a policy of apartheid in 1948 to keep blacks and whites separate? (There are several reasons, which need explanations.)

Close-ended: When did World War Two end? (1945)

Between three and six focusing questions are a good number for most historical investigations. Too few will mean not enough information. Too many will mean confusion of information.

If a piece of information you collect does not help you answer the focusing question, it is not evidence.

If a piece of information you collect does help you answer the focusing question, it is evidence.

For every piece of evidence you collect, you should show which focusing question the evidence is for.

1 Put 'focusing' or 'focus' in the following gaps to finish the sentences.

a Focusing questions help you to _____ on what is important.

b You should always see if information answers your _____ question.

c The _____ should be on matching evidence to

_____ questions.

2 Cross out the least useful focusing question in the following.

a Why did the 1981 Springbok tour of New Zealand cause conflict?
b When did the tour take place?
c What reasons did the New Zealand Government have for not stopping the tour?

3 Cross out the least useful focusing question in the following.

a How did Princess Te Puea become famous in New Zealand?
b What work did she do for Maori?
c What year did she die?

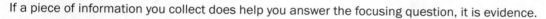

4 Underline the most useful focusing question in the following.

a How did the Velcro inventor come up with the idea and name?
b When was Velcro invented?
c Who invented Velcro?

How to plan for a historical investigation

Plan for the historical investigation = how you are going to carry out your investigation, giving details of how you will reach your goal.

Your plan could include
- focusing questions
- date for handing it in
- tasks you need to do
- timeline of milestones you want to reach
- time needed for each task
- times you will be free to work at tasks
- where you might find information
- type of information you might find
- people you might interview
- how you will make sure you do not lose your information
- helpful information such as when museums are open.

1 Highlight or circle the best alternatives in the following.

a Plan means to look ahead/to look back.

b Plans of inquiry should be the same for all students/just for the individual student.

c Organise and arrange are to do with lazy/good planning.

d 'The museum has artefacts I could examine' is an example of someone thinking about what focusing questions to make up/what type of information could be found.

e 'I need a special folder' is an example of someone thinking in a focused manner/an unfocused manner.

2 You are to do a historical investigation of a person you admire. State five things you might put in your plan for the inquiry.

_____

_____

_____

_____

3 In your own words, give the message in the lower image on this page.

_____

_____

_____

Gathering = collecting.
Selecting = choosing.

Gathering and selecting historical information means collecting and choosing material that helps you answer your focusing questions.

Examples

Maia collected her grandparents' marriage certificate and four photos of the wedding. She chose the certificate and one photo to use as evidence. She wrote on them the number of the focusing question the evidence was for and made a note in her log.

Joss collected photocopies of three tables of statistics from the town library archives. She chose one table as evidence, and wrote on it the number of the focusing question the evidence was for and made a note in her log.

Pi collected two photos of artefacts. He chose one and wrote on it the number of the focusing question the evidence was for and made a note in his log.

Phil collected information from the net by taking notes from five different sites. He chose to keep all his notes, and wrote on them the number of the focusing questions the evidence was for and made a note in his log.

1 Give the four actions all students had in common.

_____

_____

_____

_____

2 Write the note that Pi might have made in his log.

_____

_____

_____

_____

3 Fill in the gaps in the following.

Bev collected a modern atlas and an old atlas. She _____ to take

_____ of two maps from each _____ .

She _____ on them the _____ of the

_____ the evidence was for and made _____ .

How to organise historical information

Organise = to put together in a logical order, to arrange into a system.
Organise historical information = to keep all information in one place such as a folder; to put everything selected into this folder and mark the folder clearly so it is easy to see and find.

Examples of ways to organise information:

- Use focusing questions as headings and file information under them.
- File information in order of gathering and selecting.
- File information under types of sources the information is, such as interviews and net.
- File information in order of events such as 1898 Old Age Pensions Act first and 1900 Public Health Act second.
- File under headings of Most useful, Maybe useful, Least useful.
- File under location, which is the place where you collected the information.

1 State which way would probably suit you best to file information, and why.

_____

_____

2 State six ways this person could organise her historical information.

_____

_____

_____

_____

_____

_____

3 Show on the thermometer where you aim to be in organising future historical information, and give a reason for your choice.

_____

_____

_____

_____

HOW ORGANISED ARE YOU?
- IN CONTROL
- NOT BAD
- HMMM...
- A MESS!

 ISBN: 9780170389334

Rank = to put in order of importance. It is useful to also give a reason for why you ranked one piece of information ahead of the piece below and behind the piece above.

Example

Rank	Source of information and reason for ranking
1	*1920 Bloody Sunday* by H. Cork. Clear language, details, causes and results. Author is relation of 1 of 62 people wounded at Croke football stadium by British, makes account compelling but he keeps unbiased viewpoint. Answered all my focusing questions. No other source gave such quality evidence.
2	*Black and Tans versus IRA*, edited by E. Scarrow. Collection of primary sources including diary entries, interviews, newspaper stories. Shows attitudes of both sides, insight into 1920 event. Lacks excitement of Cork's book but gives more evidence for focusing questions than Irish ballads.
3	*Irish Ballads from the Anglo-Irish War*, sung by Irish Glowworms. Of the 12 ballads, 9 refer to Bloody Sunday. I can use quotes from them. Evidence sketchier than Scarrow but more colourful than 4th-ranked from the net and relates better to focusing questions.

1 What do all three things in the ranking example have in common?

_____

_____

_____

2 Give evidence the person who wrote the example understands the ranking process.

_____

_____

_____

3 To what history source, such as a movie or artefact or comic or book, would you give this award? Give at least one reason for your answer.

_____

_____

_____

_____

How to evaluate a historical investigation

Evaluate = to look at something carefully to work out its worth, to judge its quality.

Examples of questions to ask when evaluating:
- What worked well?
- What problems did I have?
- What things were easier to do than others?
- What did I like doing best?
- What did I like doing least?
- What was I most pleased about?
- Did I find enough information for my focusing questions?
- What, if anything, was I disappointed about?
- Was my information mostly useful, or mostly not useful?
- What could I have done better?
- What might I do differently next time?
- What have I learned about my skills?
- What have I learned about me?

1 Give a reason for each of the following.
  a Evaluation is a useful skill to have.

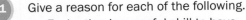

_____

_____

  b You need to be honest in your evaluation.

_____

_____

2 In each bubble, put the four questions you would ask first in your evaluation.

 ISBN: 9780170389334